Praise for *The Consciously Unbiased Educator*

Schools should be learning spaces that amplify all voices, affirm all students, and holistically position learners for academic and social success. In *The Consciously Unbiased Educator,* Huda Essa empathically guides readers to reveal and understand conscious and unconscious biases that affect personal perceptions and attitudes that lead to educational inequities. She challenges readers to bravely face, reflect on, and grapple with personal values, experiences, and histories that influence worldviews and engagement with others. As the reader is thrust into thought-provoking narrative and self-reflection activities, the book's progression opens cycles of learning and unlearning that are critical to acknowledge the intersectionality of all students. Prompting readers to extend their independent learning into collaborative, courageous conversations and see, hear, and feel the impact of their perceptions and misperceptions on the students and families they serve, *The Consciously Unbiased Educator* leads readers to honestly identify personal paradigms and systemic barriers that must be dismantled in order to spark the transformative change needed to create an inclusive, thriving culture in schools.

—**Dr. Alicia Monroe**, CEO/Founder, Solutions for Sustained Success, LLC; author of *Don't Dismiss My Story: The Tapestry of Colonized Voices in White Space*; adjunct professor, Rowan University; member, ASCD Faculty

Timely and relevant, *The Consciously Unbiased Educator* is a powerful guide that goes beyond traditional educational discourse. Huda Essa's approach is to the point and heartfelt, delivering a transformative experience that requires reflection, engagement, and, most important, action in your classroom. Through poignant examples, insightful narratives, and practical classroom strategies, the book empowers educators to embrace vulnerability, confront their privileges, address their biases head-on, and create a learning environment where openness and authenticity thrive. *The Consciously Unbiased Educator* is not just a read; it's a roadmap for transformation, urging educators to be agents of change in creating a more just and inclusive educational landscape.

—**Dr. Ignacio Lopez**, educator, educational psychologist, and author of *Keeping It Real and Relevant: Building Authentic Relationships in Your Diverse Classroom*

Huda Essa is an empathetic companion on your journey to becoming a culturally proficient educator and human. She will gently but directly challenge your perceptions and assumptions. Serving as expert, coach, and critical friend, she provides tools you'll want to revisit time and again. No matter what level of education you work in, you will want to keep this book handy.

—**Dr. Crystal Ramsay**, senior director,
Teaching and Learning with Technology, Penn State University

Huda Essa masterfully explains the importance of liberation from unjust systems by familiarizing, acknowledging, and embracing cultural influences within educational environments. She makes a compelling case for the significance of educators confronting their own biases while becoming culturally proficient and culturally responsive. Essa provides practicable tools and implementable strategies enabling educators to self-reflect, discover, and take immediate action to mitigate influences that inhibit them from seeing, valuing, and respecting the culture of every student.

—**Dr. Roberta M. Heyward**

Huda Essa bravely holds your hand as she shatters your restrictive biases and then gracefully guides you through the challenge of authentically acknowledging your own passive awareness. This is not only an educator's journey toward empowerment for themselves and their students by breaking down unjust systems, but a deeply personal expedition to awaken your truth and begin a clearer path to mindfulness. This is for the betterment of our society.

—**Nina Abadeh Ghasham**,
special education and multilingual teacher

The
Consciously
Unbiased
Educator

The Consciously Unbiased Educator

HUDA ESSA

Foreword by
Yvette Jackson

ascd

Arlington, Virginia USA

2800 Shirlington Road, Suite 1001 · Arlington, VA 22206 USA
Phone: 800-933-2723 or 703-578-9600
Website: www.ascd.org · Email: member@ascd.org
Author guidelines: www.ascd.org/write

Richard Culatta, *Chief Executive Officer;* Anthony Rebora, *Chief Content Officer;* Genny Ostertag, *Managing Director, Book Acquisitions & Editing;* Susan Hills, *Senior Acquisitions Editor;* Mary Beth Nielsen, *Director, Book Editing;* Miriam Calderone, *Editor;* Thomas Lytle, *Creative Director;* Donald Ely, *Art Director;* Melissa Johnston/The Hatcher Group, *Graphic Designer;* Valerie Younkin, *Senior Production Designer;* Kelly Marshall, *Production Manager;* Shajuan Martin, *E-Publishing Specialist;* Kathryn Oliver, *Creative Project Manager*

PAPERBACK ISBN: 978-1-4166-3278-8   ASCD product #121014   n3/24

PDF EBOOK ISBN: 978-1-4166-3279-5; see Books in Print for other formats.

Quantity discounts are available: email programteam@ascd.org or call 800-933-2723, ext. 5773, or 703-575-5773. For desk copies, go to www.ascd.org/deskcopy.

Library of Congress Cataloging-in-Publication Data
Names: Essa, Huda, author.
Title: The consciously unbiased educator / Huda Essa ; foreword by Yvette Jackson.
Description: Arlington, VA : ASCD, 2024. | Includes bibliographical references and index.
Identifiers: LCCN 2023050996 (print) | LCCN 2023050997 (ebook) | ISBN 9781416632788 (paperback) | ISBN 9781416632795 (pdf)
Subjects: LCSH: Culturally relevant pedagogy. | Educational equalization. | Teaching—Psychological aspects.
Classification: LCC LC1099 .E83 2024 (print) | LCC LC1099 (ebook) | DDC 370.117—dc23/eng/20231213
LC record available at https://lccn.loc.gov/2023050996
LC ebook record available at https://lccn.loc.gov/2023050997

33 32 31 30 29 28 27 26 25 24   1 2 3 4 5 6 7 8 9 10 11 12

This book is dedicated to my loving family and the unparalleled educator of my life, Mama. I will be forever grateful for your constant love, inspiring faith, and steady support.

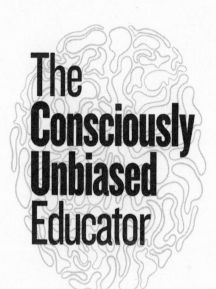

The Consciously Unbiased Educator

Foreword

The potential of the United States to maintain its role as a leader on the world stage is rooted in and contingent upon our most prolific resource: the diversity of the American people. Studies in the sciences and the arts have shown that diversity catalyzes the variety of perspectives, experiences, and strengths that spawn and optimize U.S. creativity and innovation. This reality is substantiated by the fact that "the United States, a country that accounts for about 5 percent of the world's population, has won about 60 percent of all the Nobel Prizes ever awarded. From the motor car and the airplane to Facebook and Google, from the telephone and the internet to Hollywood and Wall Street, scientists, entrepreneurs, and entertainers from the United States have powerfully shaped the world in which we live" (Vedantam, 2019).

But America has a history of ignoring and negating the incredible, undeniable influence and power of its diversity by viewing its own people's innovation through a discriminatory lens, attributing success to the intellectual ability and talent of a chosen few. The resulting prejudices and biases convey that peoples not recognized by this myopic lens lack the potential or the talent to contribute to the successes of America, perpetuating the myths about these peoples originally promulgated by racism.

However, the 20th century provided us with the cognitive science and neuroscience demonstrating that we are *all* born with the desire to be engaged; the propensity to develop high intellectual abilities, strengths, and talents; and the self-determination to succeed and make contributions. What is needed to cultivate the desire and the potential of *all* our students to learn is what all people need to succeed: exposure, enrichment, opportunity to apply critical and creative thinking, and support for high levels of learning. America abounds in the resources to provide each of these critical components, so why don't we lead the world in nurturing and eliciting the potential of our students so that they thrive and contribute to our productivity and advancements?

Tragically, the reasons are political and social rather than scientific. Enabling the potential of *all* our students requires giving them access to the aforementioned critical components, and providing this access is predicated on belief in their potential. When we believe students have talent and potential for high-level performance, we provide them with access to opportunities, resources, and pedagogy that nurture their potential and eradicate hindrances to the fulfillment of that potential. But we do not provide that access. Despite the science substantiating the power of diversity to increase U.S. innovation and the propensity of *all* students to develop the skills and talents to contribute to such innovation, the conscious and unconscious bias propagated by racism continues to influence how students are or aren't educated and, consequently, who does and doesn't achieve.

Much of the consequence of unconscious bias in education comes down to a collective lack of recognition of the reality of bias in schooling, including the behaviors that reflect it, what facilitates those behaviors, how those behaviors are manifested in teaching, and the effects those behaviors have on learning. Huda Essa eloquently elucidates this reality through the tour de force she has penned in *The Consciously Unbiased Educator.* She masterfully uses her acutely sensitive dialogical perspective acquired from empirical research and her lived experiences to curate teaching scenarios, administrative actions, and personal reflections to poignantly illustrate how bias lives in schools. Her ability to crystallize seemingly esoteric concepts from scholarship—such as *unconscious bias, cultural proficiency, privilege,* and *exclusionary behaviors*—deepen our understanding, making us keenly aware of the ideology that creates bias and the power it has to blind us to the vast and valuable potential of students who have been traditionally otherized.

The heightened consciousness that Huda deftly stimulates generates our appreciation for the pedagogical strategies, practices, and leadership moves she provides that can address and mitigate the negative impact of bias on learning. These are augmented by individual and group exercises for deep reflection that can foster our competence to make more mindful and effective pedagogical choices for enhancing the learning and achievement of *all* our students.

Huda Essa has gifted us with the pedagogical equivalent of the Hubble Space Telescope. Her book provides us with a powerful lens through which we can transcend the limitations of unconscious bias to recognize and appreciate in our students what Essa eloquently refers to as "magnificent, expanded views" of the brilliance of *all* our students, strengthening our resolve and confidence as *consciously unbiased educators.*

—Yvette Jackson, EdD

Letter to the Reader

Dear reader:

I write this at a time in history that feels unprecedented and yet, in some ways, all too familiar. It is a time of contrasts. Justice seekers are demanding change while others who are served by the status quo fiercely petition against it. On the one hand, technology is exposing long-hidden offenses like never before, and, in a few cases, has yielded long-overdue justice. On the other hand, that same unfettered access to technology has led to the widespread dissemination of misinformation, often rooted in bigoted belief systems. Legislators are enacting laws to suppress the truthful teaching of history, and heavily sanitized curricula are designed to cover up the mistakes of some and highlight those of others. Muddying the facts in this way perpetuates fragility and fear while silencing educators and diminishing the value of education. It is not an overstatement to say our rights as educators and the minds and futures of all humanity are at risk.

I have designed this text to help you more powerfully advocate for students, educators, and education itself. My hope is that with its guidance, ignorance and fear will evolve into confidence, knowledge, and empathy. Your entire community will learn to stand strong and steady upon a foundation built on character and truthful education. It is my honor to have written this book for you, my fellow influential educator, with confidence in your limitless ability not only to create waves of transformation but to teach others to do the same.

—Huda Essa

Introduction

Cultural proficiency learning is distinct among professional development subjects for an array of reasons—perhaps first among them, because it requires *un*learning as much as learning. Specifically, it requires uncovering and overcoming unconscious biases that nearly all of us have been programmed to unknowingly abide by our entire lives. This lack of awareness severely limits our potential for positive growth and impact. Conversely, raising your consciousness by gaining cultural proficiency—your goal in reading this book—will set you up to become *consciously unbiased* and therefore able to take control of what you allow to influence your beliefs and actions. The control you gain will also enhance your ability to purposefully engage in thoughts and behaviors that maximize your potential for success and that of your entire community.

What Does Cultural Proficiency Learning Involve? Who Is It For?

To deliver this content as effectively and productively as I know how, I structured this book a bit differently than most. Becoming a consciously unbiased educator requires you to undergo a deeply personal evolution, in the process gaining vast awareness, conducting soul-searching reflection, showing great vulnerability and courage, and building your stores of empathy. The thorough contemplation and resolve necessary to succeed in this undertaking will not occur through a swift read and premade checklists. Although I can empathize with busy educators looking for shortcuts, attempts to take them here will end in failure. Shortcuts support a perilous assumption that there is one exact answer for each question or problem that arises. The reality is that the world, including all the cultures and humans within it, is constantly changing. Therefore, it is imperative that you are equipped to respond as effectively as possible to *all* kinds of populations and circumstances—even communities almost entirely made up of White students. A common misconception I encounter in my work is that cultural proficiency is relevant only to teachers of ethnically diverse student populations. For reasons you'll find illustrated throughout this text, communities with the least diverse representation of identities may need this learning most of all. You will also see why an invaluable element of true cultural proficiency is learning about identities that aren't significantly represented in your classroom or even in research and data. Without this learning, your lack of knowledge about various social identities is guaranteed to show up in your practices and communications.

How to Use This Book

Because cultural proficiency benefits everyone and applies to all people, cultures, and circumstances, there will never be one set method for how to best serve your students in this ever-changing world. Therefore, I have designed this book to help you build the knowledge and skills required to become *your own manual*. Using this text, you will be able to continuously advance your skills to successfully navigate all sorts of situations, whether they are planned or arise abruptly in the moment. Countless educators were not taught to be culturally proficient, leaving them ill equipped and reluctant to respond to the issues that matter most to their students. This sends a tragic message that I have heard repeatedly from students: "My teacher's comfort is more valuable to them than my well-being."

To address this gap, the "Connect and Converse" reflection sections offer numerous opportunities throughout this book to build greater confidence and ease around speaking to sensitive, difficult matters. My sincere hope is that you exercise mindfulness and thoughtfully engage with the prompts and, in some cases, "converse" with me by reading my own reflections (indicated with an "HR" icon standing for Huda's Response). Doing so will enable you to hone your skills for independent application and transference to real-life situations rather than depending on cookie-cutter answers that have been handed to you. Most important, this practice sets you up to regularly activate your critical consciousness skills, which will help you more confidently engage in similarly important conversations off the page. To offer more space for reflection, these prompts, along with the Privilege Check-In from Chapter 4 (p. 72), are also available for download at https://www.ascd.org/consciously-unbiased-resources.

Now for a brief overview of this book. Chapter 1 is where you'll learn about unconscious bias as it relates to you personally and the ways it affects your work and the communities you serve. This chapter also introduces important strategies and tools that will help you get the most out of the book. In Chapter 2, you will learn what research and data reveal about the harmful effects of unconscious bias and delve into ways to stop shame from limiting your progress. Chapter 3 provides the background knowledge and vocabulary necessary to establish a strong foundation for future learning and growth. In Chapter 4, you'll sharpen essential skills and uncover personal learning that expands your empathy, understanding, and capabilities. Chapter 5 teaches you to activate your critical consciousness to more effectively assess and productively respond to behaviors created by prevalent unconscious bias in schools. In Chapter 6, we'll put all your learning into practice and assess how far you've come while exploring knowledge and strategies to take you further. The book concludes with Chapter 7, where I leave you with a note for what lies ahead.

A Note on Voice and Language

I'd like to touch on voice, language, and terms used in this book, since the topic is a sensitive one. As I explain more fully in Chapter 1, my own perspective is one of compassion and humility; I have tried to keep my tone warm and even light and humorous when warranted, but this book necessarily delves into serious matters that are sometimes difficult to talk about. If you are ever in doubt, please remember that I am *with* you on this journey.

I wrote this book with the intention of modeling thoughtful language. I have done my best to replace commonly used deficit-based language and labels with more precise, asset-based language. For example, I swap out *low-socioeconomic-status* or *low-income* with *underresourced*, and I replace the term *achievement gap*—which focuses on an inadequate end product—with the more accurate and productive descriptor *academic potential gap*, which addresses the heart of the matter: the way in which some students' academic potential is restricted more than others'. Both *underresourced* and *academic potential gap* focus on what can be done to lift people out of those positions rather than just imposing a label and a fixed status, which implies passivity and helplessness on the part of those being described.

Terms commonly used to describe language learners are prime examples of deficit-based language, where value is placed solely on the English language rather than the outstanding benefits of speaking more than one language. The term you'll read here is *Emergent Multilingual Learner,* which is appropriately and deservedly asset-based and inclusive of students' native and cultural languages.

While writing and revising this book, I have also rethought the common term *microaggression*, concerned that *micro* might minimize the seriousness of such an action. As a result, I have largely replaced this term with the more accurate *exclusionary behavior* (Tulshyan, 2022). My hope is that you will easily recognize both terms when you hear them used in the world beyond this book. There is no term that is "perfect," but I believe *exclusionary behavior* comes closest at this time.

I also want to discuss the terms and usage around race in this book. Race is an unfortunate social construct that provides an excuse for many to justify division, supremacy, and injustice. Although I strongly believe in honoring specific ethnicities and cultures that reside within each of these extremely broad identifiers, I can only illustrate the consequences of these made-up classifications by using the given terms. As with the term *exclusionary bias*, I have tried to choose what I believe are the best terms while acknowledging that they are not perfect (see, for example, the debate around the term *AAPI* [Kaur, 2023], which I use to refer to people of Asian American and Pacific Islander heritage). I hope that you are able to read these labels with the understanding of how incredibly diverse they are. For example, although your students who are Indigenous or Arabs may not be the first you think of when seeing the so-called "Brown" racial group, many of the obstacles they face align with those encountered by others more commonly identified in that category, such as people whose origins are from Latin America. In keeping with my use of language that is specific and inclusive of diversity, I do my best to steer away from broad terms like *people of color.* Another reason to avoid this term is that it implicitly reinforces the notion that "White" is the norm, with everyone else lumped together as a group of "other" people of "color." For this reason, among others, I have chosen to capitalize all racial identities, including *White.* Using a proper noun helps to combat the misinformed belief that White is neutral, which makes it easier to dismiss its prominent role in education, communities, and systems and to propagate misguided ideologies like color-blindness. As you read on, you'll see why this belief is pervasive and incredibly important to overcome.

I hope that considering voice, using asset-based language, and capitalizing all racial identities model inclusiveness and the meaningful effects it creates while helping you more thoughtfully and confidently engage in learning for cultural proficiency.

Now that you have an idea of what to expect and why this book is organized and written the way it is, let's get started on this journey of a lifetime!

1

Seeing the Big Picture
Embarking on Your Cultural Proficiency Journey

Instruction in youth is like engraving in stone.

—Moroccan proverb

"I am a better person today because of [*educator name*]." If you haven't made a statement like this at some point, you've probably heard some-one else say it. These memorable figures are the ones who touched our hearts, opened our minds, and awakened our souls. Many among us have the privilege of remembering such a special educator.

Of course, there are also educators we remember for the opposite reason. You may have personally experienced, witnessed, or heard stories of educators whose actions led to suffering. I am certain that most were oblivious to the ongoing effects of their actions. Their inten-tion was most likely to help, not harm, their students. Nonetheless, impact does not always match intent.

The significant longitudinal effects teachers have on student out-comes are undeniable (Johnston et al., 2019). It is therefore crucial that your positive intent is reinforced with instrumental know-how. My own intent is for the guidance throughout this book to fortify your goal of a profound legacy of excellence.

For now, though, I just want you to have hope. If you feel jaded by failures resulting from the unjust policies and practices in today's educational systems, I get it. I will not insist that you proceed filled with unwavering optimism that you will change the world (yet). Still, I trust that you know the power of knowledge. If you devote to this text the relatively short amount of time it requires, you will be rewarded with a plethora of potential positive outcomes. As you advance your professional skills, you will increase student motivation, engagement, and overall achievement. In addition, this learning will enrich your aptitude for positive collaboration and communication with not only students but also caregivers, staff, and community members. The positive effects will even extend to your personal and social life.

And to all you eye-rollers out there: I see you. All I ask is that you begin with a smidgen of hope that the knowledge you gain will enhance the overall impact of your work.

Identifying Unconscious Bias and Shame

Do not look where you fell, but where you slipped.

—Liberian proverb

If we want our students to remember us as educators who touch hearts, open minds, and awaken souls, we must boldly address the topic of bias. Discussion of its presence in school communities is often restricted to accounts of explicit bias alone. *Explicit bias* is easily recognized, and it occurs in relatively rare circumstances. It shows up in conscious, deliberate behaviors like sexist jokes, racial slurs, or refusal of service to someone of a given sexual orientation. When explicit bias occurs, the perpetrator is aware of it and can easily describe the reasoning behind it.

Although certainly harmful, explicit bias is not our biggest problem. More insidious is *unconscious bias,* also called *implicit bias*—a type of social cognition that occurs below the surface, making it harder to detect. Its origins are not so much firsthand experiences as they are societal norms and stereotypes that we unconsciously internalize. Regardless of ethical or moral attitudes and intentions, the formation of unconscious biases is a universal guarantee for all human beings. Social scientists find that unconscious biases develop as early as age 3 (Flannery, 2015). They are often undetected and may even be in direct contradiction to a person's pronounced beliefs. As a report from the Kirwan Institute (Staats et al., 2016) notes, "research from the neuro-, social and cognitive sciences show that hidden biases are distressingly pervasive, that they operate largely under the scope of human consciousness, and that they influence the ways in which we see and treat others, even when we are determined to be fair and objective" (p. 6).

Each unconscious bias we hold splashes the lens through which we see the world. Over time, these nearly imperceptible smudges are what we use to interpret what we see, draw our conclusions, and make our subsequent choices. To remain oblivious to our unconscious biases is to give them free rein over our everyday thoughts, behaviors, and communications. This obliviousness perpetuates the admission of dangerous ignorance that gives rise to enduring negative influences.

Inequities in our education systems are overwhelmingly due more to unconscious bias than to explicit bias. The disappointing reality is that most educators have been trained to provide services in a way that permits systemic oppression to continue. The sources, materials, and experiences supplied to educators are not conducive to promoting cultural proficiency. In fact, they do the opposite. Unfortunately, this truth remains widely unknown and is continually denied and dismissed by large sectors of society. Unless educators learn to recognize and mitigate their unconscious biases, their damaging effects will persist. For the sake of all former, current, and future students, we must learn to see through the false illusions our suppressive education taught us to interpret as reality.

To prevail over unconscious biases, educators need to achieve cultural proficiency. Although the journey toward achieving this goal is eye-opening and even life-changing, it rarely offers a straight and smooth path. Charting my own course toward cultural proficiency forced me to face a barrage of mortifying realizations, each one a drop of fuel to ignite embers of shame, setting them ablaze and threatening my ability to confidently advance. Fortunately, I quickly saw that giving any power to shame would threaten or even halt my progress. In hindsight, I see that my refusal to allow shame to slow me down turned out to be one of the best decisions of my life. I want the same for you.

Recognizing the presence of shame is key. This can be tricky because shame is a shapeshifter of sorts. It may appear when we least expect it or when we are least ready to face it. Shame often resides at the deepest levels of our consciousness, yet it drives many of our surface reactions. Do not mistake my words of caution as doubt in your capacity for growth; I simply want to equip you with the tools and awareness to journey toward cultural proficiency effectively and efficiently.

The first tool comes in the form of an idea that you will need to keep in mind throughout this learning: *We were all born into systems of injustice that were already in place.* Neither our formal nor our informal education taught us how to liberate ourselves from these oppressive cycles. Any missteps you have taken up to this point are not indicative of an immoral nature but, rather, of the education and conditioning you've received. Acknowledging this whenever shame threatens your progress frees up your mind and heart to appreciate the lessons that exist in that moment and amplifies your ability to practice empathy, which researchers now identify as the most important leadership skill (Brower, 2021). Among other abundant lifelong advantages, empathy fosters deep intellect, problem solving, creativity, social-emotional balance, brain functioning, and productive collaboration. It is an inarguably powerful skill for students and educators alike.

Preparing for the Journey: Creating Your Index

A fault confessed is half redressed.

—Zulu proverb

One of the most important tools I want to share is an index that you will create to help you organize your learning. Achieving the goal of cultural proficiency is a deeply personal experience that deserves a specialized approach, and as you read, you will experience an array of emotions, thoughts, and reactions that deserve moments of pause and reflection. (If you just sighed at the prospect of this taking a lot more time than anticipated, rest assured that the additional time invested upfront will accelerate your progress.) To begin, grab a notebook; this will be your constant companion and a key component to your interactive engagement on this journey. In your notebook, you will create a system inspired by Brené Brown's (2022) "integration index," itself adapted from Maria Popova's "alternative indexing" approach. Its purpose is to help you organize and reinforce your learning based on what is most useful to you.

To create the index, make a list of categories that hold the most meaning for you. You hold the pen here, so make it distinctly your own. You can add or revise categories at any time. Once you have your list, write each one as a heading on a page or two in your notebook. Make sure you leave enough blank space below each heading for your notes. Here are some examples of possible categories:

- **"Aha" moments:** New learning or information that excites or inspires you
- **Vocabulary:** Unfamiliar vocabulary words and definitions worth exploring or using
- **Quotes:** Quotations that resonate with you
- **Dig into later:** Questions, things you don't understand, ideas you want to research further and learn more about
- **Put on hold:** Concepts that you need to put on hold for now. These might be ideas that challenge you beyond your current bandwidth for whatever reason—anything from a tired mind after a long day to emotionally charged reactions like shame and fear. It is OK to press pause, but this category is your promise to yourself to revisit the concepts so that you won't have gaps in your foundational learning.
- **Talk it over with _____:** Ideas that you want to share and discuss—for example, with colleagues at a meal, with loved ones on a call, with students in class, or with followers in a social media post

- **Take to work:** Takeaways for timely application
- **Schedule it:** Actions that you don't want to forget to take
- **Personal connection:** Ideas that ignite empathy on any level. This could be in ways that relate directly to your life experiences or to those of significant others, including but not limited to ancestors, admired figures, family, and friends.

Far from being just another task, the index enables you to obtain learning in the way that is most meaningful to you. It asks you to slow down and distinguish ideas that resonate with you, including ones that upset, excite, or perplex you. You can highlight and tag notable ideas, recording the page number and any relevant notes under the corresponding index category.

An Invitation to Connect and Converse

Constant dripping hollows out the stone.

—Vietnamese proverb

Another key tool I offer in this book involves conversation. Free, honest conversation is crucial to our cultural proficiency journey. And once again, shame rears its head as a major roadblock to this kind of open discourse. One of the subtlest manifestations of shame is what I call the "programmed hush." This is not the silence associated with captivated engagement; it is the silence derived from disconnectedness between people, which leads to feelings of insecurity, inferiority (or superiority), uncertainty, inadequacy, stress, intimidation—even spite, anger, or apathy. Maybe the disconnect is between you and your colleague, your doctor, or the keynote speaker on stage—whoever it is, the missing ingredient is empathy. Empathy is needed to generate the comfort necessary for authentic and productive discourse.

The next tool is going to help you overcome the programmed hush. Here is how it works. Throughout the book, I pose questions that prompt you to reflect on an aspect of the information shared or how it applies to your life. I urge you to record your unadulterated, genuine responses in your notebook. Some of these may be sobering, but don't hold back. Withholding truths may deal a less severe blow to your ego, but it shoves you backward on your journey. Who has time for that? Not you! If you feel stuck on a particularly challenging question, you can add it to a "Put on hold" section in your index, but you will need to revisit it at some point, so it's best to complete as much as you can before moving on in the text. Once you have written your response, go to the page listed next to HR (standing for Huda's Response). There, you will read my response, which may include any combination of personal narrative, researched facts, and alternative perspectives that you may or may not relate to personally.

Now here is the real challenge: I want you to do your best not to peek at my responses before you hash out your own thoughts. Otherwise, you will remove your voice from the conversation and rob yourself of the opportunity to learn in a deeply personal way. Including your unfiltered voice expands your knowledge base and gives you practice breaking the programmed hush instigated by shame. Engaging in our conversation here will infinitely enhance your experiences off the page. You can then use your acquired skills in a way that compels others to do the same. To help you in this endeavor, I have purposely placed my responses apart from the prompts, at the end of each chapter.

A note on the "voice" of my responses: I want you to "hear" them in a compassionate voice. (If you've ever sent a text message that was wildly misconstrued, you will understand this request!) Because this book is likely to kindle an array of emotions, I want to be clear about my intended voice. It is not one of judgment or arrogance, but one of humility, empathy, and genuine care. In my consultations with professionals, I intentionally maintain a relaxed and informal atmosphere and dialogue. Here, I offer you a similar opportunity. I'd like you to indulge in the notion that although I am not physically in your presence, my written responses are what I would say to you in person. And while it is true that I won't receive your responses in the moment, my genuine hope is that you and I will meet face-to-face in the near future. Until then, rest assured that my hearing your response is nowhere near as important as you expressing and really listening to your own voice. You will soon see why understanding what *you* think is the most effective action you can take.

Finally, I have provided multiple opportunities for you to reflect on and expand your worldview. You will see that many of these *don't* include a response from me. This varied approach is designed to allow you to learn in a more natural, authentic way, meaning sometimes you'll be able to talk it out to learn more, and other times you'll need to expand your knowledge in other ways. These might include conducting intentional research through various modes of media, engaging in conversations with others, or acquiring accurate information from observations made through your enhanced, clearer lens.

Let's start this practice by returning to the beginning: childhood. Psychology professionals agree that a great deal of our anguish stems from this time in our lives. Many of my own childhood memories are from Michigan in the late 1980s and early 1990s. Smartphones and online social media did not exist. Neighbors sat on their front porches and visited one another frequently. Kids played in the streets until sunset. We drank from hoses without a second thought and used them to spray unsuspecting siblings and friends during the humid summers. My memories include elaborate hairstyles, heavily trafficked sidewalks, and highlighter-bright colors. However, this particular memory I'm thinking of includes simple hair and shades of dull brown: my neighbor Penny's brown brick house, with its oak front door, coffee-colored mailbox, and wheat-brown stucco lining the front porch steps and columns. The sneaker-scuffed, drab brown tile on the floor stands out the most. The day my heart broke and my chin dropped, that floor is what I stared at through a curtain of brown hair that I let fall to hide the tears stinging my chocolate-brown eyes.

Just moments before, we had been excitedly planning an epic sleepover at Penny's. It would involve braiding each other's hair, giggling over magazines, and eating buttered popcorn. With ear-to-ear smiles, Jill and I wiggled and hopped with excitement, waiting for Penny to return with her mother's permission. We were sure the answer would be yes but were still eager to hear the joyful confirmation. The door swung open, and out came Penny skipping toward us. She enthusiastically announced to Jill that her mom had said yes! They swung their linked hands as they squealed and jumped up and down. As if on cue, Jill's mother called to her from across the street to let her know that supper was ready.

I was stirring with excitement for my turn to celebrate with Penny as she watched Jill run home. After what seemed like a long time, she turned to face me, and I saw that her smile had disappeared. "Umm, Huda, we need to talk." My bubbly friend's voice had instantly transformed into an adult-like tone. She gently took my arm and walked me to the edge of the porch. Her eyes seemed to glance everywhere but my face as she mumbled, "My mom said you can't sleep over." Confused, I replied, "But you just told Jill that your mom said yes." She took a deep breath, and this time, she looked straight at me to say, "My mom said that Jill can sleep over but you can't because you're Black." Confused again, I said, "I'm not Black, I'm Arab." With a look of pity and a slight shake of her head, she said, "It's the same thing." I felt like I had been punched in the gut. My throat tightened and I turned my face toward the dusty brown floor. Now I was the one who couldn't look at her. Heartbroken and filled with shame, I walked the short distance home. This was not the first time I had faced racial discrimination in my short years, but when it came from loved ones, it pierced through the thick skin I was rapidly growing to protect myself.

As teenagers, my siblings and I would laugh at this story. By the time I became a culturally proficient adult, the memory would come back to tug at my heartstrings all over again. I grieved Penny's spoiled sense of unreserved love and that of all the souls taught to hate. I held an acute sadness for my younger self who, like so many of us, trusted in the oppressive, atrocious lie that Black was somehow bad. But above all, this memory fills me with determination to turn both types of victims into champions.

CONNECT AND CONVERSE

> › Think back to your childhood years. When did you first con-
> template race, and what prompted this? (See **HR1** on p. 22.)
> [HR]

> › What notions did you absorb about each racial identity?
> Some responses may be obviously stereotypical or biased,
> but I urge you to honestly think about them anyway. (See
> **HR2** on p. 22.) [HR]

Look Back to Advance Forward

Do not fear a stain that disappears with water.

—Puerto Rican proverb

Revolutionizing unjust education systems requires comprehending how and why unconscious bias directs our beliefs and actions. My story echoes those of countless others who have similarly embarked on the journey toward cultural proficiency.

Once again, allow me to press the rewind button and return to my childhood years. Unbeknownst to me then, my adolescence bore witness to White flight and the ways it reformed the neighborhood I called home. Before then, my family was one of a small number of Muslim and Arab families in the area. We did not look like most families there or the staff at my school. We were bilingual, bicultural, and Brown. From a young age, my mind absorbed endless messages that taught me what was good versus bad, what was acceptable versus unacceptable, and what was deemed "normal."

In my very first years of schooling, it became quickly and painfully clear to me that my family and I were *not* normal. Compared with most of my classmates' names, mine was unusual and difficult for my teachers to pronounce. My parents were immigrants, and their English didn't sound like that of most other parents. Even the lunch I brought from home was not like my friends'. Plain and simple, I was different and I knew it.

The evidence of what was normal and the glaring notion that I was *abnormal* were continually confirmed through nearly every channel and experience of my youth. Literature was a big one. I was an avid reader as a child. As is true for many readers, I swiftly became submerged in the books I read. My imagination delighted with every new character and storyline I encountered to the extent that I *became* the character. This was not fun for my family, especially when the character was a young detective or an up-and-coming musician. My now enhanced lens allows me to see that reading was not just an outlet; it was a coping mechanism by way of dissociation. Reading was my chance to escape my excluded reality and live vicariously through characters that were "normal."

The diversity of the U.S. population was increasing, but you wouldn't have known it looking at children's literature at that time. It hardly ever included anyone other than White, able-bodied, monolingual, Christian characters, so the message of what constituted normalcy was loud and clear. To take just one data point, in 1990, only 51 of an estimated 5,000 children's books published were by Black authors and illustrators (Cooperative Children's Book Center, 2023). This was consistent with other forms of media I consumed. In TV, film, popular magazines, news media, advertising, school curriculum, and even the toys I played with, narrow and biased representation endured. Although the characters represented in these media had a variety of problems, rarely were they related to the systemic injustices that I, like nearly all children with excluded identities, was forced to grapple with. Like these characters, most of my classmates and school staff were not frequently obliged to feel inferior or contemplate identities such as race, ethnicity, language, or religion. Those with widely represented identities benefited in countless ways. When your people's diverse stories are widely shared by *your* people, it is a prevailing privilege most others can only wish they had. Those with excluded and misrepresented identities face a barrage of destructive consequences likely to persist through lifetimes and generations.

Cultural proficiency affords me the insight to understand how harmful it was for me to be exposed to such limited perspectives. One of the most profound psychological effects was an aching, continuously unfulfilled longing to fit into a mold that was not created for the likes of me. My integral human need to feel a sense of belonging was unrelentingly threatened. My adolescence was shaped by a constant struggle to fit into a concrete mold, to show others that I was not all that different—that I, too, was a normal American (Essa, n.d.). My learned unconscious biases dominated my motivations, from the ways I spoke and thought to how I acted, dressed, and styled my hair. Although I couldn't yet understand why and how this was the case, I was acutely aware of how utterly exhausting it all was.

However hard this marginalization was for me and others like me, an individual injustice leads to a collective loss for us all. My experience had a compounding effect on my entire community, including those with widely represented identities. Imagine the breadth of useful knowledge that could have been gained from embracing the diverse identities, cultures, and places of origin represented in the community. In not doing so, the community unknowingly blunted the attainment of lifelong skills like empathy and critical consciousness.

The disadvantages of this marginalization go even further. In the United States, I find that many need to be reminded that unless their ancestors were Indigenous to this land, they are all descendants of people whose origins began elsewhere. As society does to Brown and Black people and people of AAPI heritage today, centuries of oppression robbed my White neighbors, classmates, and teachers of the invaluable gift of knowing their own origins. The beneficial attributes of their heritage, such as language, traditions, family, and world history were buried. (I discuss this more extensively in subsequent chapters.) These losses are all our losses. We are all deprived of the informational wealth that could have been gained from an abundant array of cultural knowledge and skills.

Billions of people throughout the world have unfortunately received a formal education devoid of such high-quality learning. No one is immune, yet everyone can improve. In the United States, the greater majority was deprived of what Dr. Rudine Sims Bishop (1990) beautifully describes as follows:

Books are sometimes windows, offering views of worlds that may be real or imagined, familiar or strange. These windows are also sliding glass doors, and readers have only to walk through in imagination to become part of whatever world has been created and recreated by the author. When lighting conditions are just right, however, a window can also be a mirror. Literature transforms human experience and reflects it back to us, and in that reflection, we can see our own lives and experiences as part of the larger human experience. Reading, then, becomes a means of self-affirmation, and readers often seek their mirrors in books. (p. ix)

Bishop is referring to literature, but this passage could just as easily apply to curricula, instruction, and school cultures. Every student, past, present, and future, deserves this sort of education. The learning you do throughout this text will help you obtain and offer this education.

Review, Reflect, Resolve

If we wonder often, the gift of knowledge will come.

—Arapaho proverb

The most substantial progress often occurs outside the keynote, PD workshop, or, in this case, the pages of the book. It transpires when you apply the knowledge attained to your everyday life, both in and out of the classroom. To help you get started, the conclusion of each chapter takes our "conversation" to the next level with one more tool: a set of three prompts designed to expand your understanding of the chapter. First, I ask you to simply *review* your perspective of the topic presented. To expand your comprehension, you are then prompted to *reflect* more deeply on your experiences, beliefs, and relevant impacts. Last, you will *resolve* to immediately apply your learning toward improved practices and continual growth.

These 3*R*s, as I refer to them, supply you with opportunities for contemplation and guidance for actions that move beyond your thoughts and into the real world. I illustrate this method more thoroughly in

Chapter 5, but for now, just know that the 3*R*s help you build independent practice that will prove useful over time. Don't forget to use your personal index to help you power through more productively!

Review

- Think back to your childhood. Were you exposed to people, curricula, and media that offered you "mirrors, windows, and sliding doors" to a diverse array of identities and perspectives? (See **HR3** on p. 23.) HR
- When did you take notice of whether you shared the racial identity of leaders and figures you learned about in your curricula and most media sources?
- Are you aware of whether your family history is like that of most others in the United States? Might it include instances of encountering prejudice or using tactics to avoid it that resulted in the loss of identities and valued cultural traits?

Reflect

- What are some advantages to young people seeing people who look like them in influential and positive roles?
- How have your experiences with and among diverse populations shaped your worldview?
- What obstacles have you faced due to limited knowledge of diverse identities (e.g., discomfort around discussing various topics, lack of confidence communicating with and learning from various identities, unhelpful and misplaced shame or fear)?

Resolve

- Consider the disadvantages you now have owing to discrimination your ancestors may have encountered. These may include loss of invaluable assets like languages, cultural traditions, family history, lessons, recipes, and communications, along with less direct disadvantages like poorly developed empathy.

- If this history is unknown, look into why information relating to your ancestors' identities is unavailable to you—for example, is your family or ethnic history unobtainable or unknown, were your ancestors forced into enslavement, did your family change their name due to discrimination, did your family lose native language(s) that your ancestors may have spoken, or is your family unable to understand or practice cultural traditions that were once invaluable to your ancestors?
- Discuss your findings and the emotions that arise from them with at least a few others to compare and learn from one another's stories. It is best if you have access both to people who apparently share your racial identities and to those who do not. No matter their identities, engaging your colleagues in these prompts is an opportunity to plant seeds of knowledge, empathy, and motivation. Inviting others on the journey with you will only increase your capacity.

When spider webs unite, they can tie up a lion.

—Ethiopian proverb

Huda's Responses

 HR1:

Think back to your childhood years. When did you first contemplate race, and what prompted this?

My anecdotal experiences consistently imply that Black and Brown people and those of AAPI heritage tend to think about race from a very young age. Research confirms this finding and expands on its associated detriments (Dulin-Keita et al., 2011). Reasons for this awareness abound, from facing or witnessing differential treatment and misrepresentation to being taught ways at home to prepare for and protect themselves from racism. Race becomes a dominant identity considered frequently for the rest of their lives.

 HR2:

What notions did you absorb about each racial identity?

Regardless of our own racial identities, we are all susceptible to social conditioning that teaches us a notion of separatism and supremacy (Perszyk et al., 2019). Until my early 20s, I lived in complete ignorance of the innumerable biases I personally held. As a result of the relentless advocacy of some educators at my university, I was finally offered the incomparable learning opportunity I never knew I was missing. Dr. Leslie Thornton's course, focused on cultural competence, paved the way for me to eventually learn firsthand how unconscious bias had shaped my thoughts, feelings, and actions in countless ways. Rather quickly, my learning illustrated the many ways in which I have served as both the oppressed and the oppressor. Because I identify with several marginalized identities, my self-identification as oppressor comes as a surprise to many. But a vital acknowledgment is that *everyone* holds unconscious biases. In fact, a great many of us hold *shared* widespread biases, regardless of our identities and backgrounds. This is primarily because main-stream media, curricula, and systems exposed us to many of the same overarching notions. For disenfranchised communities, the damaging effects are twofold because they include uphold-ing negative beliefs about our own identities as well as others.

HR3:

Think back to your childhood. Were you exposed to people, curricula, and media that offered you "mirrors, windows, and sliding doors" to a diverse array of identities and perspectives?

I can without a doubt say that the missing mirrors, windows, and sliding doors produced tidal waves in my world. I have already shared some impacts of absent mirrors in my early learning. Here, I want to elaborate further on the significance of the severely lacking windows and sliding doors. They were a major factor in why I did not have a great deal of empathy for others who faced similar disenfranchisement. Simply put, my formal education perpetuated unconscious biases that inhibited my ability to build essential empathy skills.

Every single one of us deserved an education that provided us with the mirrors, windows, and sliding doors necessary to draw the most excellent educator out of each of us. I will not blame my previous teachers, though. They taught me what they were taught, and what most educators in the United States were taught: the sweepingly biased version of history. This version includes "discovered land" and "peaceful Thanksgivings" where the Indigenous people were "savages" who were "civilized" by the supreme colonizers. If only my teachers and, consequen-tially, my classmates and I, had been taught the *truthful* perspec-tive, we might have developed invaluable critical thinking skills and empathy. As a descendant of refugees, I would have found special meaning in the truthful history about the origins of the land I now live on. Like the Indigenous peoples of North Amer-ica, my ancestors were native to the land where they, too, were subjected to brutal colonization and ruthless ethnic cleansing. Backed by supremacist ideologies, both groups were murdered or forced out of the homes, communities, and land that they and a long line of their ancestors had cultivated. Both groups were then and are still portrayed as savage and uncivilized to justify collective punishment and elimination among even the youngest among them. Both persecuted groups' past and present tragedies and struggles are suppressed and distorted alongside attempts to erase or undermine their existence.

The commonalities of these two heart-wrenching stories could fill the pages of this book, but my point is this: had I been taught the truthful perspective about the Indigenous peoples of the land I live on today, I would have developed the empathy to understand *their* story as *my* story. Instead, the false, one-sided education I received taught me what it likely taught you and every other student: to recognize people as "others." Instead of inclusive learning opportunities that taught us to see and benefit from our common humanity, the learning my teachers and I received produced exclusionary beliefs and behaviors that we acted on without a second thought. It contributed to my classmates and me regularly playing "Cowboys and Indians"—and you can guess who the bad guys were. Considering the particularly personal empathy I could have easily accessed makes that memory both ironic and poignant.

I feel privileged to have gained knowledge that enables me to identify and improve upon these and other misguided beliefs. My realizations fostered what is now a genuine, acute empathy for South Africans, Uyghurs, Venezuelans, Bosnians, Rwandans, Iraqis, Black Americans, Rohingya, Brazilians, and virtually all previously or currently oppressed peoples. My knowledge has made me a vastly more qualified educator and a stronger advocate for the trustworthy, empowering education that we *all* deserve.

My dawning consciousness of my limited beliefs led me on a quest to continue deepening my understanding of how it was

I could be so insensitive. I learned how I could be devoid of empathy for those who faced discrimination that was so similar to mine, and why it took so long for my awakening to occur. My path toward cultural proficiency uncovered tangled roots of injustice that ran deeper than I could have ever imagined. It also revealed what should have been taught to me far earlier in my education: that I carry an untapped potential to make waves in what may appear to be injustices set in stone. I *could* create reverberating change. I am here to tell you that you have that power as well.

2

Examining the Problem
What Research Tells Us About Unconscious Bias

The one that plants thorns must never expect to gather roses.

—Arab proverb

In this chapter, I delve deeply into what research and data reveal about the harmful effects unconscious bias has on students with marginalized identities—principally Black, AAPI, and Brown students, as well as Emergent Multilingual Learners—and the negative outcomes these students can expect throughout their lives as part of what I call this *unconscious bias cycle*. Because data isn't the final word on this topic, I also look beyond the data at certain factors it doesn't address. Finally, I explore how the information shared in this chapter can equip you as a shield against shame and move you one step closer toward cultural proficiency.

Labels: A Breeding Ground for Bias

Awareness is the key factor to overcoming unconscious biases; without it, the fabric of our school communities will deteriorate. Believe it or not, symptoms of these biases may appear in the relationships between teachers and students *before they even meet*. The following is an example from my own experience at a staff meeting in a school I used to work in.

Our school staff gathered at the end of summer break, radiating rejuvenation. Colleagues strolled into the room with refreshed smiles, sun-kissed faces, and new stories to tell. Laments about the summer having moved too fast were balanced with eagerness to jump back into a steady routine. Everyone took their seats with the optimism of a fresh start. Then class rosters were distributed, and silence enveloped the room. As eyes rapidly scanned the lists of student names set next to an alphabet of identification labels, reactions ranged from pleased smiles to thoughtful concentration to heavy sighs. The room soon buzzed with chatter. My attention was seized by the quiet but blunt voice of my neighbor. Her index finger skimmed down her class list as she read, "ESL, ESL, at risk, ESL, special ed, at risk, ESL, retention, special ed, at risk... and, of course, almost all low-SES, or so their families *claim* to be. I bet at least half the parents can't even speak English, or they work full-time themselves, so I have to be the miracle worker—or else. It isn't the kids' fault, but it's so unfair that I'm going to be evaluated based on working with this group. My friend is a teacher in 'Richville,' and her problems are *nothing* compared with what we deal with, yet I'm going to be evaluated the same way she is. How in the world is that supposed to be fair?"

This sort of dialogue transpires in school communities around the globe. Whether spoken outright or in covert terms, educators frequently subscribe to the notion that assigned labels are conclusively accurate and complete descriptions of their students. This doesn't happen in a vacuum. As Yvette Jackson (2011) observes,

> The prejudging practice of sorting students based on standardized criteria evolved from the government's need to expedite and facilitate classifying students without the expense of training teachers to assess the learning potential of the students. Education became the only field in which requirements or mandates were not followed by explicit training based on research about the stated objective—reversing underachievement.... This governmental practice of control through classification of students set

off development of a chain of marginalizing labels that fostered misperceptions about students, in turn perpetuating a cycle of prejudicing belief and lower expectations. (p. 19)

As long as this cycle continues, educators are destined to accept what they are given: inaccurate or incomplete information that tightens the hold of unimpeded, damaging unconscious biases.

 CONNECT AND CONVERSE

> How do members of your school community perceive and respond to labels (e.g., ESL, at risk, special education, retention, low-SES)?

> Do these current attitudes toward student labels support and empower students in those groups, or do students encounter lower expectations and end up fulfilling them?

(See **HR4** on p. 42.) [HR]

Unconscious biases can produce a mismatch of intent and impact in several important areas. For example, research on educators' unconscious biases around gender (Chemaly, 2015) shows that up to two-thirds of teachers' time is spent talking to male students. When teachers ask questions, they more frequently direct their eyes on boys and call them to the front of the class for demonstrations. They reward girls for being quiet while encouraging boys to seek deeper answers. If you feel confident that this would never describe your own actions, know that the teachers studied felt the same way. The research found that teachers remained unaware of their imbalanced treatment until they viewed their videotaped interactions. This lack of awareness has resounding outcomes: in the classroom, girls are more likely to be interrupted and boys allowed to talk over them. This much-studied norm perseveres well into adulthood, where it can be witnessed in professional and social settings (Hancock & Rubin, 2014).

Conceptions around gender roles in occupations appear to be formed around age 4. The U.S. education system weakens boys' interest in language and the arts and girls' interest in math and science performance, which results in "the United States holding one of the world's largest gender gaps in those subjects" (Chemaly, 2015). In addition to women, people with marginalized ethnic and racial identities are also underrepresented in STEM and computer science, with unconscious bias as a contributing factor (Dee & Gershenson, 2017). Again, this points to unconscious biases' influence on who we believe is most capable and who belongs in which careers. The cycle steers cultural norms that can be observed within the United States, the United Kingdom, and Canada.

These biases create glaring absences in these fields that nevertheless have stood the test of time. Plainly put, if you don't see it, you won't be it. Other countries have much higher proportions of women in science and engineering (Bernhardt, 2014), such as Trinidad and Tobago, Azerbaijan, Tunisia, Thailand, and Armenia. When people witness women represented in these careers, it helps set the norm. This representation provides mirrors to girls so they may see themselves reflected, showing them possibilities to achieve the same.

Confined Views Confine Potential

Fear an ignorant human more than a lion.

—Kurdish proverb

Unbalanced representation and the unconscious biases it leads to weaken the many beneficial effects of diversity. The demographics of U.S. educators reflect this imbalance, and they transcend generations. Consider the educators you, your teachers, and your teachers' teachers were exposed to in U.S. schools. I'm guessing nearly all these teachers and principals were White. Research bears out this anecdotal data: although the majority of U.S. students are not White, about 79 percent of teachers are (National Center for Education Statistics, 2021). The clear imbalance remains similar in higher education, where about 74 percent of faculty are White (National Center for Education Statistics, 2022). This demographic is often maintained in the portrayals of educators in literature, television, and film. Unconsciously, we are being told which identities best suit the role of educator, and so the status quo remains unchanged. As you read, I want you to keep one fact at the forefront of your thoughts: *Anyone, of any race, can be an exceptional educator when effectively taught to be one.*

Diversity in the teaching force benefits *all* students. Without that diversity, cultural proficiency is even more crucial. Unfortunately, cultural proficiency remains a low priority in informal and formal education systems alike. Compared with their Black, AAPI, and Brown colleagues, White educators are almost certain to have less real-world experience with discrimination based on race or ethnicity. Although many White educators have ancestors who suffered injustices due to biases around their ethnicities, most now live in a society that is far removed from that past. This disconnect leaves them vulnerable to picking up and acting on culturally destructive notions that do not serve them or their students. Attaining cultural proficiency without guidance is hard enough for all educators; doing so without personal experience of the damaging effects of unconscious biases takes the difficulty up a notch.

CONNECT AND CONVERSE

> Did most of your teachers and principals share your racial identity?

> Did your education prepare you with the diverse guidance and perspectives necessary to obtain a culturally proficient skill set? (See **HR5** on p. 43.)

The unconscious bias cycle depicted in Figure 2.1 illustrates how the lack of formal or informal education in cultural proficiency fosters continuous negative outcomes for Black, AAPI, and Brown students. After you have read through this cycle, I want you to engage in a quick empathy skill builder. Take a moment to consider the following prompts:

> How might a similar cycle exist for other marginalized identities? For example, you might focus on women in STEM and computer sciences.

> How do the outcomes of cycles like this create problems for you personally? For education systems? For the world?

Figure 2.1. Unconscious Bias Cycle

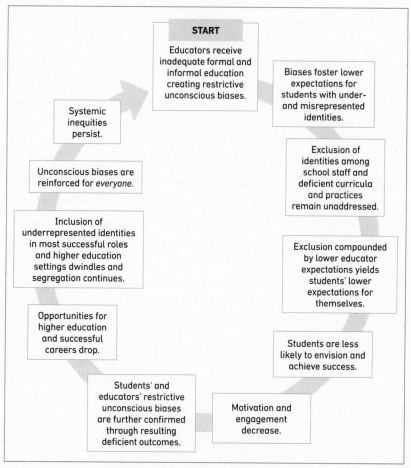

Source: Used with permission of Huda Essa. © 2024 Huda Essa.

Research supports the existence of the unconscious bias cycle, showing that unconscious racial bias is one of the biggest barriers to closing the academic potential gap between White students and Black, AAPI, and Brown students (Harrington, 2018). Educators' unconscious biases lead them to project lower expectations onto and provide less support for their Black, AAPI, and Brown students (Castillo et al., 2019) and contribute to these students having negative experiences with their teachers and being at a higher risk for school failure (Van Den Bergh, 2010).

We know by now that representation matters. Student-teacher racial mismatch increases the likelihood that a student will be chronically absent, which can decrease their development of literacy skills by 14 percent in kindergarten. In the 4th grade, chronic absenteeism contributes to around 17 percent of the academic potential gap between White and non-White students (Holt & Gershenson, 2015). Research (Ouazad, 2014) shows that on average, Black and Hispanic elementary students are more likely to receive lower grades from White teachers than from same-race teachers.

Conversely, having at least one same-race teacher results in improved performance (Lindsay & Blom, 2017). Compared with their non-Black colleagues, Black teachers are 12 percent more likely to expect Black students to complete a four-year college degree (Gershenson et al., 2016). Grissom and colleagues found that Black or Hispanic students, even those with high test scores, are referred to gifted programs significantly less frequently than their White peers, but Black students being assigned to gifted programs in both math and reading is three times more likely to occur when their teachers are also Black (Grissom & Redding, 2016), and schools with larger numbers of Black and Hispanic students in gifted programs correlate with higher numbers of Black and Hispanic teachers (Grissom et al., 2017). The statistics are borne out in higher education, too: in community colleges where faculty look more like their students, performance gaps among racial identities can narrow by 20–50 percent (Fairlie et al., 2014).

Sometimes unconscious bias emerges in subtler ways. Some White teachers may believe that they are "rescuing" their Black, AAPI, and Brown students. This so-called "White savior" complex might make the teachers feel good, but it stems from toxic notions that non-White cultural backgrounds are inferior (Endres & Gould, 2009; Howard, 2010; Pennington et al., 2012). Another insidious unconscious bias that might seem harmless on the surface is the conception of Asian Americans as the "model minority," which contributes to stereotypes, minimizes or invalidates Asian Americans' own experiences of racism, and creates unrealistic academic expectations (Boiko-Weyrach,

2017). Moreover, this arbitrary "ranking" of racial identities appears to place Asian Americans above their Black and Brown counterparts, threatening to create resentment and contempt. Rather than increasing solidarity and probabilities for shared success, then, this absurd notion only widens the divide between people of marginalized identities, thereby limiting everyone's potential.

Research indicates that disproportionate disciplinary actions are taken toward Black and Brown students in general, as well as students with disabilities. Sadly, the disparities prove once again how bias-driven actions are linked to lasting outcomes, in this case unemployment (Pager et al., 2009) and criminal involvement (Hirschfield, 2009). The U.S. Department of Education Office for Civil Rights (2014) collected data from every public school in the United States that supports the argument for helping educators attain cultural proficiency:

- Black children represent 18% of preschool enrollment, but 48% of preschool children receiving more than one out-of-school suspension; in comparison, white students represent 43% of preschool enrollment but 26% of preschool children receiving more than one out of school suspension. Boys represent 79% of preschool children suspended once and 82% of preschool children suspended multiple times, although boys represent 54% of preschool enrollment.
- Black students are suspended and expelled at a rate three times greater than white students....American Indian and Native-Alaskan students are also disproportionately suspended and expelled....
- Black girls are suspended at higher rates (12%) than girls of any other race or ethnicity and most boys; American Indian and Native-Alaskan girls (7%) are suspended at higher rates than white boys (6%) or girls (2%).
- Students with disabilities are more than twice as likely to receive an out-of-school suspension (13%) than students without disabilities (6%).
- While black students represent 16% of student enrollment, they represent 27% of students referred to law enforcement and 31%

of students subjected to a school-related arrest. In comparison, white students represent 51% of enrollment, 41% of students referred to law enforcement, and 39% of those arrested. Students with disabilities (served by IDEA) represent a quarter of students arrested and referred to law enforcement, even though they are only 12% of the overall student population.

• Students with disabilities (served by IDEA) represent 12% of the student population, but 58% of those placed in seclusion or involuntary confinement, and 75% of those physically restrained at school.... Black students represent 19% of students with disabilities served by IDEA, but 36% of these students who are restrained at school through the use of a mechanical device or equipment designed to restrict their freedom of movement. (p. 1)

Similar disparities affect Emergent Multilingual Learners. Note that these students are commonly referred to as English language learners (ELL) or students learning English as a second language (ESL). As noted in the Introduction, it is important to replace these commonly used labels that focus on deficits with more precise, asset-based terms. The use of deficit-based language to describe these resourceful learners is just one of the many restraining impacts of unaddressed unconscious biases. The following data provides some examples of the many disparities encountered by this student population (Artiles & Ortiz, 2002).

• When compared with their peers who only speak English, Emergent Multilingual Learners are 15–20 percent more likely to leave school before graduation.

• Over- and underrepresentation of Emergent Multilingual Learners is common in district special education programs throughout the United States. Disproportions are clear in comparison with their monolingual peers.

• Emergent Multilingual Learners with the greatest probability of referral to special education programs are those with the least language support in school. In contrast to Emergent Multilingual Learners receiving some native language support, those confined to instruction in English alone were nearly three times as likely to be placed in special education programs.

This data reinforces the main idea woven throughout this chapter: knowledge is power, and that power has been withheld from most educators for too long. Changing the status quo for all marginalized populations requires educators to receive a culturally proficient education. Only then will they be able to create an authentically equitable and inclusive learning environment. This is how teachers of *all* identities will most effectively support students of all identities. Students' backgrounds can be utilized as the rich assets they are, enabling students to be more engaged, motivated, and successful learners.

Expanding Vision Beyond the Data

Justice delayed is justice denied.

—Albanian proverb

Data provides concrete examples of how unconscious biases affect actions and systems. Helpful as this is, though, tunnel vision around the individual identities researched can prevent us from seeing the bigger picture. It is imperative to acknowledge that a great number of other vulnerable identities may not have the backing of research or definitive numbers to support their similar experiences. This does not negate the fact that the obstacles they face very much exist and are worthy of serious consideration. Even in the collection of data, discriminatory and oppressive policies create unnecessary limitations. It is usually those with personal experience of these limitations who are aware of them, of course. This is true for numerous identities, including some that I identify with.

Millions of Arab Americans along with hundreds of thousands of Iranian Americans live and work in the United States. They don't personally identify as White, and they certainly are not referred to or treated as such. Yet whenever their race is formally questioned for documentation and data collection, these individuals are required to identify as White. For decades, community nonprofit organizations and state agencies have made appeals to get this right. Outcomes include substantial, thorough testing administered by the U.S. Census Bureau that led to recommendations for these groups to be more accurately recognized, yet this right continues to be denied. As a result, the countless contributions the people in these groups make to the country they live in are disregarded and unaccounted for. Excluding their identities from data and studies distorts statistics and minimizes educators' and service providers' abilities to improve practices and relationships. In addition, it deprives these groups of minority status that, in some cases, could provide the equity necessary to help them overcome obstacles they encounter as a marginalized group.

Another factor rarely accounted for in data is regularly occurring religious discrimination. Granted, acquiring information on such discrimination can be tricky, but leaving it unaddressed guarantees its continued existence. This certainly remains true for Muslim students, yet very little research around the matter has been published, although efforts are being made to bring more data to light by groups such as the Council on American-Islamic Relations (2023) and the Institute for Social Policy and Understanding (Mogahed et al., 2022). The regular downplaying of its importance discourages certain groups from reporting hate crimes when they occur. Like others who face discrimination for more than one identity, Muslims sadly become accustomed to prejudice and bullying. Adding insult to injury, their reports are frequently dismissed as exaggeration or hypersensitivity. This appears to be especially true when there is severely limited data available to support the testimonies. All these factors strongly diminish the likelihood that targets of hate incidents will report them when they occur. In a study of U.S. Muslims' perceptions of Islamophobia in the United States, more than half of respondents reported that they had personally experienced an Islamophobic incident but did not report it to the authorities (Elsheikh & Sisemore, 2021). Most Black, AAPI, or Brown people would understand this, as would women who have reported sexual harassment or assault only to face scrutiny and blame afterward.

Just as increasing awareness of learned biases around race, gender, language, and physical and learning abilities is important, educators must attain religious literacy as well. Research indicates that familiarity with a given religion leads to warmer views of it. Warmer views create openings for consciously unbiased learning, enhanced community-building efforts, and greater achievement for all. Whether or not you have students of different religious identities in your community isn't important; your knowledge, or lack thereof, about these key social identities is sure to appear in your practices and communications.

Educators wanting to take control of their unconscious biases refuse to remain ignorant about the topic. Given that there are thousands of religions throughout the globe, it is safe to begin with basic knowledge around the largest populations. Islam is currently the second-largest religion in the world, and its followers include individuals of all ethnicities and races. Still, this immense population continues to be misunderstood. Perhaps the most relevant data would be that collected among the general U.S. population, which, of course, includes school community members. Extensive research shows that "Americans remain unfamiliar with Islam; feel more coldly toward Muslims than any other religious group; and tend to see Islam as 'more violent' than other religions" (The Bridge Initiative, 2015, p. 6). In the same study of U.S. Islamophobia cited above, 97.5 percent of participants believed that portrayal of Muslims in U.S. mainstream media is unfair (Elsheikh & Sisemore, 2021). These impressions are supported by research: rampant misinformation and negative stereotypes are consistently perpetuated by Western media (Samari, 2016). These are compounded by heavily biased news reports (Elmasry, 2015) as well as fictional TV shows, movies, and books, which significantly shape our understanding of the world. U.S. writer Jack Shaheen (2001) shared the evidence found in his examination of more than 100 years of Western media in his book *Reel Bad Arabs*, later presented in a documentary of the same name (Jhally & Earp, 2006).

The products of such biased representation are severe xenophobia and injustice without consequence. The subsequent ignorance creates hate and fear that threaten enlightenment. Merely learning or teaching basic facts about the identity held by literally billions of humans has many times incited an angry backlash. Increasing understanding and dispelling misconceptions around this identity is one of the most popular learning opportunities I provide in my work as a cultural proficiency educator. But those whose xenophobia overpowers their will to learn are ferociously opposed to overcoming these misconceptions. Words like *indoctrination, terrorist,* and worse are tossed in my direction and that of any who choose to base their beliefs on facts.

Willful ignorance and hate are planted in school curricula where Muslims' exceptional contributions to the world are almost wholly excluded. Although we rely on and benefit from so many inventions and innovations introduced by Muslims, these remain untaught and ignored. From the coffee you drink and the toothbrush you use to the numbers you write, the hospital you visit, the planes you fly in, and the university you attended—all these and so much more originated with Muslims. As with other oppressed identities, the adverse stories we *are* told elicit unsettling fear and hatred instead of a mutually beneficial open attitude.

These skewed, fear-based stories are relayed in mass media as well. Award-winning actor Riz Ahmed takes on roles that defy stereotypical representation of Muslims. In a 2021 video titled *Muslim Misrepresentation in Film,* his impassioned plea to media creators easily extends to educators and applies not just to Muslims but to all excluded and misrepresented communities:

> I ask myself, if I'm the exception to the rule, what must the rule be about people like me? What must the unwritten rule be about Muslims, a quarter of the world's population, and their place in our stories, our culture, and their place in our society, if any?... Exceptions don't change the rules. Exceptions, if anything, they highlight the rule, and in some ways, allow us to be complacent about leaving that rule in place. The progress that's being made by a few of us doesn't paint an overall picture of progress if most of the portrayals of Muslims on screen are either nonexistent or entrenched

in those stereotypical, toxic, two-dimensional portrayals. I think we're going to look back at this period of misrepresentation with the same shame and sadness that we look upon minstrelsy in days gone by. It's something that has to be changed and it's something we can't change on our own. It's a structural problem. We have to join hands. What rewrites rules isn't exceptions but it's when the oppressed and the oppressors—whether they're aware of being oppressors, or aware of their complicity in the oppression or not—join hands, open their eyes, and make a solemn commitment to take some concrete steps. Maybe that's not just a Muslim struggle, maybe that's all of our struggle as storytellers to afford all of us that empathy and that humanity.

I couldn't agree more. Though he doesn't use the actual words, Ahmed reinforces the importance of providing all students with "mirrors, windows, and sliding doors."

As you continue to learn about the effects of unconscious bias on named groups, make sure to acknowledge marginalization that likewise affects unnamed groups who may encounter similar disenfranchisement. This awareness will enable you to more effectively foster learning environments and opportunities that are inclusive and equitable for *all*.

Moving Past Shame to Get Ahead

It is not enough to learn how to ride; you must also learn how to fall.

—Mexican proverb

I have had the privilege of working with thousands of educators who appreciate the importance of diversity in schools. Although their appreciation is sincere, however, not all educators are good at recognizing their own unconscious biases (Van Den Bergh, 2010). This is especially true for White educators, who are more likely to exhibit behaviors rooted in unconscious bias than are their Black, AAPI, and Brown colleagues (Schlosser, 2017). This is one outcome of a system that doesn't prompt them to contemplate their own racial identity, contributing to their lack of inclination to attain cultural proficiency. Again, feeling shame or taking offense would be a waste of time because this is merely the unjust system we were all brought into. Let's take control.

Interrupting ruinous cycles requires acknowledging how unconscious biases shape educators' perceptions and lead them to maintain and even widen the academic potential gap (Ferguson, 2003). A culturally proficient educator has a far better chance of maximizing student achievement and achieving professional success than one who lacks cultural competence. Thus, it is imperative that you resist the pull of shame and the reactions it sets off. If denial, anger, defensiveness, or self-pity creep up, that's just shame tapping on your shoulder and trying to push you down.

To rally against shame, use the knowledge you've gained as your shield. An uninformed person may see data indicating that Black and Brown students have lower achievement scores than White students and take it at face value, seeing race as the only contributing factor. With a clear lens, you would see that this denies the whole truth, which includes a range of oppression that led to those outcomes. You now know that one of those critical issues in educational inequity is the lack of cultural proficiency. You've learned how systemic inequities have prevented educators, particularly White educators, from gaining this life skill. The good news is that you can become a culturally proficient educator. No matter what your race or other identities are, you can ensure that you do not contribute to the negative consequences endured by so many students.

Review, Reflect, Resolve

Even if the truth is buried for centuries,
it will eventually come out and thrive.

—Filipino proverb

Review

Consider your thoughts and emotional reactions to the data provided in this chapter. Have you rejected or dismissed any of the findings because you find them hard to believe or accept?

Reflect

- How do your responses to this data confirm either the high quality or the shortcomings of educator preparation programs?
- What outcomes have you observed in school communities that might have resulted from insufficient cultural proficiency?

Resolve

- Tune in to the ways labels are used in your school community. Are they used to increase or decrease expectations? If so, for whom?
- Observe whether members of your school community confidently approach topics pertaining to bias, equity, and inclusion.
- Actively listen to and learn from people who share experiences and perspectives about injustices they have encountered. Remember that just because you don't face the same injustices doesn't mean they don't exist for others.
- Develop your empathy skills by seeking commonalities among various identities, including your own—for example, challenges faced by immigrants and marginalized groups that are similar to those your ancestors may have faced.

You make the road by walking on it.

—Nicaraguan proverb

Huda's Responses

 HR4:

How do members of your school community perceive and respond to labels (e.g., ESL, at risk, special education, retention, low-SES)? Do these current attitudes toward student labels support and empower students in those groups, or do students encounter lower expectations and end up fulfilling them?

Continual identification of students with labels develops an emphasis on shortcomings or weaknesses. Dr. Yvette Jackson (2011) explains how this originated and led to a destructive cycle:

> The prescriptive practices that were spawned by policies that mandated control... were driven by a *lack* of belief either in students or in their teachers, or most often both. Such control was negative in the way in which it deconstructed or destroyed inspiring, engaging instruction, causing disengagement, arrested growth, or even growth that atrophied, leaving students perpetually disenfranchised. (p. 19)

The significance of teacher expectations is substantiated by longitudinal research observing students' progression over the course of their school careers (Alvidrez & Weinstein, 1999). The researchers found that teacher expectations of a preschooler's ability were a strong predictor of the child's high school GPA.

Most principals and teachers agree that setting high expectations for students can have a major impact on student achievement. In addition, most teachers are confident in their ability to help all their students succeed academically. Yet in a 2009 survey of U.S. educators, only 36 percent of teachers and 51 percent of principals said that *all* their students can achieve academic success (MetLife, 2010). The negative effects are most striking in the achievement, performance, and behaviors of linguistically diverse students and those with marginalized racial identities. The well-known Education Longitudinal Study of 2002 conducted by the National Center for Education Statistics found that Black and Hispanic students were believed to have less than half the chance of getting a college degree than their White peers.

With the vast majority of teachers believing that students are simply not motivated to succeed academically (MetLife, 2010), it could appear that this has nothing to do with educators and everything to do with student engagement. But the unsettling reality is that teacher expectations are more predictive of college success than most major factors, including student motivation and student effort (National Center for Education Statistics, 2002). The reduced achievement that results from low teacher expectations feeds into a vicious cycle of diminished student outlooks, attitudes, and motivation to succeed. These examples are just an ounce from the heavy weight of unconscious biases that constrict educator and student potential. Clearly, labels—and the conclusions we draw from them about our students—matter.

 HR5:

Did your education prepare you with the diverse guidance and perspectives necessary to obtain a culturally proficient skill set?

Amplified by predominantly White-authored curricula and media, U.S. education programs are almost solely taught from the perspective of a White American. This is not to say that this view is without value or undeserving of consideration; it just shouldn't be the *only* perspective we are exposed to. Placing every one of us at an inarguable disadvantage, this centuries-old trend disregards all other identities that make up the majority of the human population.

This deficient education is exacerbated by life experiences rarely compelling White educators to contemplate the topic of race. Understandably, these educators are not lining up to expose their lack of knowledge. Research confirms the concerns that scores of dedicated educators have shared with me year after year. White educators tend to avoid discussions of race and racism in the classroom (Haviland, 2008; Ruggles-Gere et al., 2009), often for fear of saying the wrong thing (Keengwe, 2010). However understandable, the fact that race and ethnicity are one of the most significant predictors of students' academic achievement and outcomes (Jones et al., 2020) means that we need to get past this reluctance. Pervasive avoidance of the topic among educators annihilates any prospects for improvement.

Enduringly segregated communities also undermine our teacher preparation programs. Entering teacher preparation programs with little or no exposure to different cultures is common among White preservice teachers (Howard, 2010; Keengwe, 2010). When this lack of exposure is combined with one-sided media and education, it is no surprise that White educators are likely to adopt a "color-blind" approach to teaching (Peters et al., 2016). Color-blindness is a racial ideology that essentially denies the existence of racism. This sows a belief in meritocracy—that success is based solely on hard work (Howard, 2010)—thereby ignoring the long-term sociological impact of oppression and racism and sustaining the status quo (Gushue & Constantine, 2007; Howard, 2010). Hence, the denial of racism is itself a form of racism.

The color-blind approach, an incomplete worldview due to sheltered life experiences and exposure to one-sided media and education programs, and other systemic failings in teacher education programs contribute to widespread reports of dissatisfied White graduates. They accurately conclude that their programs inadequately prepared them for the realities faced in the field (Cross, 2003). White teachers' lack of familiarity with diverse racial and ethnic identities is apparent in their teaching styles, curriculum, classroom practices, and interactions with Black, AAPI, and Brown students (Cross, 2005; Fasching-Varner, 2012;

Ruggles-Gere et al., 2009; Zamudio, 2011). Education program graduates' culturally deficient education renders them unable to effectively address and utilize the assets of students' cultural backgrounds in their practices (Cross, 2003).

3
Looking Inward
Your Beliefs and Practices on the Cultural Proficiency Continuum

A tattoo cannot be made without blood.

—Mozambican proverb

Now that you are well versed in the consequences of unconscious biases, let's fill your power reserves with more of the background knowledge and vocabulary necessary to create real, lasting change in your community and beyond. In this chapter, I provide an overview of the cultural proficiency continuum and of culturally responsive practices, and you'll assess where you stand in terms of your current beliefs and practices. Then I describe three critical steps you need to practice to move toward cultural proficiency: unlearning, learning, and diversification.

The Cultural Proficiency Continuum

Let's start by looking at Figure 3.1, which depicts the cultural proficiency continuum, with cultural destructiveness at one end and cultural proficiency at the other (Lindsey et al., 2003).

Figure 3.1. Cultural Proficiency Continuum

Cultural Proficiency

Cultural Competence

Cultural Pre-competence

Cultural Blindness

Cultural Incapacity

Cultural Destructiveness

As you read the following definitions and examples of each point along the continuum, mark items that represent actions you have taken with an *X*; ones you have witnessed in your school community with an *O*; and those that you have both witnessed and acted out with an *XO*. Be sure to practice shame resiliency to protect your progress. Remember, you can only reach cultural proficiency through courageous honesty and humility.

Cultural Destructiveness: Suppression of cultures outside the dominant, privileged one.

Examples:

_____ Stereotypes and belittles nondominant cultures.

_____ Refers to various dialects of English as unintelligent, improper, or inadequate.

_____ Identifies natural hairstyles and cultural dress of underrepresented groups as unacceptable.

_____ Shortens students' names or renames them so that they have Eurocentric names.

_____ Rejects or is bothered by the use of languages other than English in the classroom.

_____ Provides limited or negative representation of nondominant cultures.

_____ Perceives learning around diversity, equity, and inclusion as indoctrination or a radical measure that threatens the privileges of the dominant group.

Cultural Incapacity: Conviction in the superiority of one culture above all others; intolerance of ambiguity, thereby reducing the ability to respect differences among cultures, which may yield oppressive actions and responses.

Examples:

_____ Is unwilling to make sincere efforts to correctly pronounce unfamiliar student names.

_____ Feels resentment toward learning focused on diversity, equity, and inclusion.

_____ Holds the belief that marginalized people should leave or "go back to their own country" rather than questioning the system that disenfranchises such communities.

_____ Blames underachievement on students' families and cultures instead of on failing systems and educators' low expectations.

_____ Attributes limited family involvement to the inferiority of marginalized cultures and identities.

Cultural Blindness: Belief or attitude that cultural differences and social identities are insignificant or nonexistent.

Examples:

_____ Makes false statements such as "I don't see color. I only see humans."

_____ Minimizes oppression of marginalized peoples by accusing them of dishonesty or hypersensitivity.

_____ Disapproves of equitable practices to instead maintain the notion that equal is fair.

_____ Ignores evidence of systemic injustices and ardently adheres to the myth of meritocracy.

_____ Disregards current realities to maintain the belief that the oppression of disenfranchised populations is history and no longer relevant.

_____ Refuses to acknowledge that unearned privileges result in abundant advantages to be enjoyed only by select groups.

Cultural Pre-competence: Superficial acknowledgment of the value of cultural diversity; having an awareness of one's limitations to achieving cultural competence yet still being unable to effectively utilize cultural diversity as an asset.

Examples:

_____ Is willing to actively participate in some but not all discussions around equity and inclusion.

_____ Learns and uses a few words in Emergent Multilingual Learners' home languages to support relationship building.

_____ Honors marginalized identities at designated times rather than inclusively throughout the school year (e.g., limiting discussions around Black history to Black History Month).

_____ Demonstrates tokenism through posters in the classroom or hallway that show diverse identities that are not more fully incorporated in the curriculum or teaching practices.

_____ Confines opportunities to learn about various cultures at the surface level only (e.g., holding a potluck event to share foods from different cultures but not using students' cultures to connect to daily learning).

Cultural Competence: Authentic practice of fundamental equitable and inclusive actions that foster an appreciation for cultural diversity; eagerness to learn in active pursuit of cultural proficiency.

Examples:

_____ Openly acknowledges the many ways one's identities, cultures, and society contribute to one's worldview.

_____ Recognizes how one's worldview shapes communications, practices, and the ability to effectively understand others.

_____ Shows willingness to learn about the ways one's privileges influence one's experiences and outcomes.

_____ Openly acknowledges the fact that one's unearned privileges have yielded advantages not granted to those in marginalized groups.

_____ Is eager to gain professional development toward attaining cultural proficiency.

_____ Makes concerted efforts to build deep relationships of mutual respect with students and caregivers of all backgrounds.

_____ Engages students in an effective, culturally responsive, and relevant curriculum.

_____ Recognizes and acts on the need to provide differentiated, equitable instruction to skillfully meet students' various needs.

_____ Creates an environment of inclusion and respect for all identities.

Cultural Proficiency: Highly developed ability to learn about individual and organizational cultures, productively interact and teach in a variety of cultural environments, and employ diversity as an asset to increase achievement of all stakeholders; active advocacy for equity and inclusion in all areas, including authentic development of cultural proficiency.

Examples:

_____ Applies and elevates culturally competent actions while incorporating advocacy that models and promotes such practices.

_____ Shows humility to effectively and authentically learn from various cultures and topics related to diversity, equity, and inclusion.

_____ Creates learning opportunities centered on fostering students' cultural proficiency.

_____ Models and teaches advocacy skills to all stakeholders.

_____ Unremittingly works toward an equitable, inclusive, and socially just school community.

_____ Understands and accepts that cultural proficiency is a life-long pursuit for continuous advancement of knowledge and capacity.

💬 **CONNECT AND CONVERSE:**

> Did any descriptions or examples along the continuum surprise you? If so, what about them did you find surprising?

> What are the sources of the beliefs that led to the actions in the checklists?

(See **HR6** on p. 63.) [HR]

You may find that the statements you noted an *X* for fell under more than one category along the continuum. The key is to distinguish why each action is classified as it is and consider how to "upgrade" it. Acknowledging where you are now and having the will and taking action to improve are essential throughout this process. As shown in Figure 3.1, the continuum's arrow points upward because there's no stopping point with cultural proficiency; it is a lifelong skill that can be stretched and improved through learning, experience, and wisdom.

Are Your Culturally Responsive Practices Destructive or Proficient?

You can outrun what is running after you,
but not what is running inside of you.

—Rwandan proverb

Contrary to what many believe, culturally responsive practices are not a supplement to your teaching; they are the guiding force. The reality is that culturally responsive teaching has always occurred and continues to occur in your school and every classroom, every single day. As Gloria Ladson-Billings (2009) puts it, "All instruction is culturally responsive. The question is: to which culture is it currently oriented?" (p. 198).

A critical component in achieving cultural proficiency is using culturally responsive practices to support your students. Effective use of this approach incorporates "the cultural knowledge, prior experiences, frames of reference, and performance styles of ethnically diverse students to make learning encounters more relevant to and effective for them" (Gay, 2010, p. 31). The irrefutable power of culturally responsive instruction isn't just backed by teacher and student testimony; it's backed by neuroscience. Zaretta Hammond's (2014) research illustrates its phenomenal impact on student participation, academic rigor, and overall student achievement: "Think of culture as software for the brain's hardware. The brain uses cultural information to turn everyday happenings into meaningful events. If we want to help dependent learners do more higher-order thinking and problem solving, then we have to access their brain's cognitive structures to deliver culturally responsive instruction" (p. 22).

Now, there is no readymade manual for culturally responsive instruction, nor should there be. This learning needs to be radically personal, because it *is* radically personal. However, by reading and responding to this text and building your own skills and practices, you won't need to depend on a written guide. Your own knowledge and experience will become your manual—one that is personal to you and tailored to your community.

As you solidify your base of knowledge around the factors that shape your beliefs and practices, it is imperative to maintain the understanding that intercultural skills—the ability to productively communicate with anyone you encounter across cultures—benefit *all* students of *all* backgrounds. Without that understanding, initiatives for culturally responsive or relevant education often fall flat and elicit hostile reactions from already overwhelmed educators. My experience has shown that this usually isn't because they are against the idea itself but because they believe it's something that both creates more work for them and only benefits students who are not White. This could not be further from the truth.

Race and ethnicity are certainly tied to distinct cultures, but they are not the only cultures to keep in mind. Every single one of us is constantly engaged in and influenced by numerous cultures and subcultures. Each of these cultures involves norms that indicate what is deemed acceptable and unacceptable. Nearly all social identities—including age group, organizational role, family, language, and religion—have corresponding cultures. Cultures can be small and localized, or they can be expansive and broad, like those recognized in whole continents and nations. Norms vary in the same way—they can be broad or narrow. Norms can vary regionally or within cities, neighborhoods, even individual homes. Your school district has norms that differ from those in the school district one city over. The same goes for school buildings, grade levels, and single classrooms. The policies, environment, leadership, and participants in a community influence the culture in particular ways. This concept also applies to cultures like athletics. Shared and distinct cultural norms are common among athletes, their families, and fans. In other words, cultural norms can be witnessed in any sphere involving human activity or interaction. As Hammond (2014) sums it up, "Culture, it turns out, is the way that every brain makes sense of the world" (p. 22).

Figure 3.2 is a depiction of the iceberg model of culture, a now commonly used metaphor showing how many aspects of culture are above and below the surface. The model includes major themes that are present in all cultures, supplying you with an invaluable intercultural skill set. The ability to recognize these major themes increases your awareness of the variances across cultures, which fosters continually enhanced understanding and communications with people of all backgrounds. Intercultural skills help you become adept at expertly acquiring useful information from every culture you encounter.

Cultures are intricate, dynamic, influential, and constantly evolving. Regrettably, many communities remain fixated on surface culture alone. This shortsighted focus produces narrow understandings of cultures that are apparent in countless well-intentioned communities whose definition of multiculturalism is displayed exclusively through basic, superficial elements. Inarguably, food, art, and language are wonderful ways to connect with and learn from one another, and events or initiatives focused on surface culture can be a part of initiatives aimed at developing community. They just shouldn't be the *only* ones.

Figure 3.2. The Iceberg Model of Culture

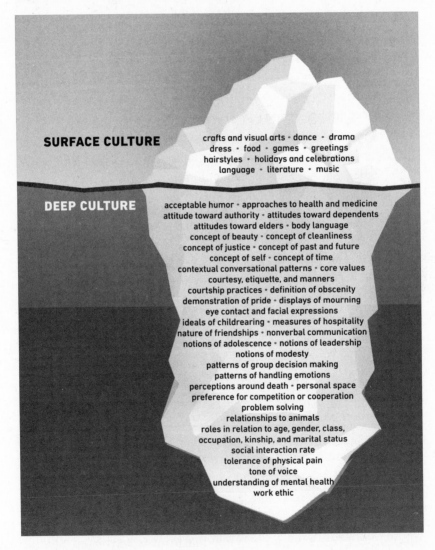

SURFACE CULTURE

crafts and visual arts · dance · drama
dress · food · games · greetings
hairstyles · holidays and celebrations
language · literature · music

DEEP CULTURE

acceptable humor · approaches to health and medicine
attitude toward authority · attitudes toward dependents
attitudes toward elders · body language
concept of beauty · concept of cleanliness
concept of justice · concept of past and future
concept of self · concept of time
contextual conversational patterns · core values
courtesy, etiquette, and manners
courtship practices · definition of obscenity
demonstration of pride · displays of mourning
eye contact and facial expressions
ideals of childrearing · measures of hospitality
nature of friendships · nonverbal communication
notions of adolescence · notions of leadership
notions of modesty
patterns of group decision making
patterns of handling emotions
perceptions around death · personal space
preference for competition or cooperation
problem solving
relationships to animals
roles in relation to age, gender, class,
occupation, kinship, and marital status
social interaction rate
tolerance of physical pain
tone of voice
understanding of mental health
work ethic

The most integral elements of culture are found below the surface. This is where beliefs and notions that strike people on an emotional level can be found. The beliefs and practices at this level are what hold authority in the lives of nearly all people. Differences among these beliefs drive thoughts, words, actions, offenses, and defenses. If you really want to build authentic relationships and mutual success, this is the place to be.

Venturing below the surface optimizes your capacity for cultural proficiency and fruitful communications. Take the highly influential norms related to "patterns of group decision making" or "preference for competition or cooperation." Both are tied to the overarching value of individualism versus collectivism associated with various national cultures (Hammond, 2014). The United States' dominant culture is individualistic (Hofstede et al., 2010), differing significantly from the collectivism of many U.S. students' home cultures, which are often aligned with their families' ethnic origins. With the exception of Greece, the countries shown to highly value norms focused on collectivism are all located in Africa, Asia, Latin America, and the Middle East (better described as Western Asia) (Hammond, 2014).

Let's zero in on this concept, beginning with its relevance to U.S. educators, most of whose origins are of European descent. This is highly relevant in classrooms, where these values oppose one another in many ways. For example, where individualism is "competitive" and "technical," collectivism is "collaborative" and "relational." Whereas individualism promotes "learning that happens through individual study and reading," collectivism upholds the belief that "learning happens through group interaction and dialogue." Where individualism "emphasizes self-reliance and the belief that one is supposed to take care of [themselves] to get ahead," collectivism "emphasizes reliance on the collective wisdom or resources of the group and the belief that group members take care of each other to get ahead" (Hammond, 2014, p. 26). Adhering to norms embedded in European or White dominant culture means abiding by rules and beliefs that are highly individualistic. Stir in formal and informal learning that is mostly from and about White people, and the outcome is all U.S. educators being influenced by this dominant culture to some degree, no matter their race. The highly likely outcome is the perception that other cultures are inadequate (Howard, 2010) and an insistence that White dominant culture is the norm (Fasching-Varner, 2012).

Whether unconscious or explicit, these views become apparent in teachers' beliefs and expectations (Howard, 2010; Zamudio, 2011). Students from cultures whose views and practices around certain norms differ from the U.S. "default" (such as collectivism versus individualism) are often misunderstood and end up being regularly reprimanded or punished. The data you explored in Chapter 2 revealed disproportionate disciplinary actions that occur in part due to unconscious biases around cultural norms. Becoming a keen observer and learner about your beliefs around cultural norms requires you to look around and within. As Jackson (2011) puts it, "When we understand the impact our cultural frame of reference has on our own behavior, we better appreciate and can respond to the influence our students' frames of reference have on their learning and their motivation" (p. 46). This practice will grant you consciously unbiased insight that will enhance your practice and your students' learning experience.

Steps on the Way to Cultural Proficiency

You cannot climb to the mountain top
without crushing some weeds with your feet.

—Ugandan proverb

Now that you have a better idea of where your beliefs and practices stand on the continuum, I want you to be aware of the overarching process for continual improvement. The path toward cultural proficiency requires practicing three critical steps:

1. Unlearning—Identifying and correcting learned biases
2. Learning—Acquisition of information, knowledge, and wisdom
3. Diversification—Increased collective capacity (Cross, 2003, p. 12)

In the following sections, we'll explore what taking these steps looks like.

Step 1: Unlearning—Acknowledge, identify, and correct learned biases.

Unlearning is the key to unlocking the door to a life of clarity, wisdom, and empowerment. By responding to the reflection prompts provided in this book, you have already taken this first step. The path may feel more like a winding roller coaster than a surefooted stroll in the park, but the rises and falls are necessary for both remedy and prevention. As you continue, armed with abundant self-compassion and humility, the shakiness and low points of this ride will dissipate. As you master assessing the quality of your beliefs, your wisdom-led actions will prevent most avoidable obstacles from cropping up. On the rare occasion that they do, your responses will be far more successful and far less stressful than they were before you started this journey. You might even find that these obstacles appear less like obstructions in your path and more as opportunities to help you strengthen your power to be and do better.

Step 2: Learning—Acquire new, improved knowledge and information.

This book provides strategies to follow up your unlearning with upgraded, superior learning. Each amended concept you learn extends your critical consciousness skills and helps you become sharply attuned to identifying and overcoming previously formed biases. This skill set enables you to take operative control of what you *allow* to influence you. You will be able to cut off the development of damaging biases, leaving you more headspace for truth and compassion. You are becoming your own manual—using your own hard-won learning and wisdom to tell you how to act and respond productively in each and every situation.

Step 3: Diversification—Increase collective capacity.

Diversification is the last step of the journey toward cultural proficiency. At this stage, you are perpetually increasing your wisdom and allies to expand your knowledge, abilities, and reach. Your collective capacity for cultural proficiency increases as you acknowledge that this is a journey of lifelong learning. Your advanced empathy skills aid you in seeking true understanding with humility, and you confidently and productively respond to both troubles and triumphs. The outcome is the type of leadership and collaboration that garners well-deserved respect.

A final thought to bear in mind is that the professional learning offered here is unlike most. It more closely resembles other intimate and collective human experiences and growth and, therefore, does not necessarily follow a linear path. Don't be surprised if you bounce back and forth between steps.

Here's an example. Let's say our conversation around the myth of meritocracy strikes a chord with you, and you make a note in your index, which then prompts you to research the systemic disenfranchisement of Black Americans. The facts and narratives you discover foster the unlearning of your previously held notions about meritocracy. Later, upon sharing your findings, a colleague contributes further information that adds to your learning. Another colleague jumps in with a reference to how the ideas relate to unfair access to education around the world, which draws your attention to another bias. The unlearning and learning process that occurs with your colleagues is more organic and immediate than the previous one; what your colleague shares makes sense and is easily proven. The discussion continues, and you find yourself bouncing back and forth between learning and unlearning all over again. Your administrator jumps in and suggests a schoolwide activity to raise awareness and advocacy around equitable access to education. On your way home that day, you feel fulfilled by your sharing that has led to copious unlearning, learning, and even diversification. Your thoughts are interrupted by someone cutting you off in traffic. Upon seeing the culprit, a questionable bias pops up in your mind. And the hop-around dance begins again.

This is just one example. You will soon have your own examples as you learn to fall in love with this soul-satisfying dance. As in life, the early "youthful" stage of gaining cultural proficiency is filled with unsteady yet fast-paced steps. Later, wisdom earns you the privilege of a poised slow dance that establishes a deeper footprint.

Review, Reflect, Resolve

Every head is a world.

—Cuban proverb

Contrary to popular belief, cultural proficiency does not begin with learning more about the community you serve. It is a key element, to be sure, but not necessarily the most useful *first* step to take. Instead, an effective understanding of your community requires that you first have a profound, multifaceted understanding of who it is *you* are.

So before you join a crowd, I invite you to first dance alone in the mirror. Dancing solo allows you to constructively comprehend the complex and deeply intricate factors that shape your worldviews. You'll start by taking a closer look at your social identities and the ways they inspire your beliefs and subsequent behaviors.

Review

1. In Figure 3.3, fill in how you believe you fit each of the social identities listed.
2. On a scale of 1–10, rank how often you think about each identity (1 = rarely, 10 = many times a day).
3. Circle the identities you think about the most.
4. Draw an X through the ones you think about the least.

Figure 3.3. Your Social Identities

Age		Race	
Ethnicity		Native born/ Nonnative	
National origin		Geographic location	
Language		Communication style/skill level	
Mental/ physical ability		Learning ability	
Emotional ability		Neurological identities	
Religion/ spiritual affiliation		Biological sex	
Gender identity/ expression		Sexual orientation	
Income		Work experience	
Occupation		Education	
Appearance		Family	
Parental status		Partnership status	
Political beliefs		Military background	
Addiction/ recovery status		Any other significant identities?	

CONNECT AND CONVERSE

Reflect

> Which experiences or beliefs cause you to think about the social identities you circled the most?

> Why might certain identities come to the forefront only in specific situations?

> Why might particular instances or environments diminish your consideration of regularly contemplated identities?

> Why do you contemplate the lower-ranking identities less often than others?

> How are your actions and beliefs shaped by your social identities?

> How do others' positive perceptions of your identities affect your actions and reactions?

> How do others' negative perceptions of your identities affect your actions and reactions?

(See **HR7** on p. 64.)   [HR]

Resolve

- Become more observant of the cultural norms and social identities that appear to be most favored and most widely represented in influential positions, curricula, and mass media.

- Pay attention to pronounced or nuanced benefits that present themselves as a result of broad representation and/or positive perceptions around some of your identities. These benefits might include greater acceptance, higher expectations, diminished prospects of stereotype threat, feeling comfortable and safe in most places, and so on.

- Look back at the checklists aligned with the cultural proficiency continuum (pp. 47–51). Beginning with just one or two noted items on the checklists, jot down improved actions that you'll replace them with moving forward.

– In your planner or go-to device, create a reminder to revisit the list and your resolution. If your intention was unfulfilled, commit yourself to getting it done. If you did accomplish your goal, acknowledge and praise your job well done. Then select the next one or two actions to improve and repeat the process.

To be willing is only half the task.

—Armenian proverb

Huda's Responses

 HR6:

Did any descriptions or examples along the continuum surprise you? If so, what about them did you find surprising? What are the sources of the beliefs that led to the actions in the checklists?

If the checklists following the cultural proficiency continuum surprised you or your ego took a hit, know that this is not uncommon. Taking the temperature of where you stand today is a vital part of this process that will become easier over time. It allows you to better see where the mismatch of your intent and impact manifests.

To illustrate, let's take the example of *cultural blindness:* the belief or attitude that cultural differences and social identities are insignificant or nonexistent. When I was younger, I used to make all types of assertions that promoted the myth of meritocracy. Yes, I had bought into the lie I was taught: that outcomes and success are almost wholly based on merit and abilities. Even when my own personal experience and observations proved otherwise, I couldn't shake the belief. Time and time again, ability and effort nearly always lost inside corrupt systems where notions of supremacy reigned. My unchecked unconscious biases directed me to blame myself, making my struggles that much harder. My severely deficient empathy skills expanded the victim blaming to other oppressed identities as well (although I thought I was giving helpful advice). Rather than concentrating on the systemic forms of oppression that were the source of the inequities, I insisted that "those people" just needed to work harder, do more, be more.

Once my eyes were finally opened to the myth of meritocracy, I was able to advance a step further on the continuum. It was there that I began stumbling upon a great number of unpleasant surprises. Although many were humbling truths

about my own beliefs and actions, about an equal number highlighted the senselessness accepted widely by society. Cultural
blindness serves many illogical claims that people defiantly
defend. Saying things like "I don't see color, I just see people" is
simply a lie. Yes, we do see color. Denying this obvious fact is an
act drenched in privilege that hurts us all. Sticking to this idea
permits rampant ignorance so that uncomfortable truths can be
avoided. Moreover, the false claim disregards the experiences of
those regularly harmed by discrimination and exclusion.

If this was a tough pill to swallow, know that it won't be your
last. But I promise that it will eventually happen far less. Ultimately, the blips of temporary discomfort will yield a priceless
sense of confidence and liberty.

[HR] HR7:

**Which experiences or beliefs cause you to think about the
social identities you circled the most? Why might certain
identities come to the forefront only in specific situations?
Why might particular instances or environments diminish
your consideration of regularly contemplated identities?
Why do you contemplate the lower-ranking identities less
often than others? How are your actions and beliefs shaped
by your social identities? How do others' positive perceptions of your identities affect your actions and reactions?
How do others' negative perceptions of your identities
affect your actions and reactions?**

The identities we think about most are those that have the
greatest impact on our beliefs and experiences. The effects of
holding those identities vary by environment. For example, let's
say someone identifies as transgender. It is highly likely that this
identity is one they think about a lot. Their day-to-day experiences and emotions are influenced by their sense of belonging
or lack thereof, which results from others' perceptions and
feedback. The effects of adverse reactions can be especially
strong and will influence this person's future behaviors, such

as minimizing their expression and increasing anxiety, which hinders otherwise normal communications. By contrast, these disadvantages are nearly eliminated in settings perceived as more inclusive and among others who share this identity.

Meanwhile, this same individual may have inherited substantial financial wealth. There is a great deal of comfort and ease within this identity. In most environments, responses to this identity are consistently positive. Therefore, this person may find little need for contemplation around it. The occasional moments that do inspire additional thought often result from the presence of people or ideas that serve as reminders of this privilege. Even then, such moments don't occur often enough to foster enduring contemplation.

These concepts and more are further unpacked in Chapter 4, where I share information and examples to expand your comprehension around the reflections from this chapter.

4

Moving Forward

*Finding the Courage to Be Vulnerable
and to Confront Privilege*

The one who tells the stories rules the world.

—Hopi proverb

In Chapter 3, you viewed your beliefs and practices through the lens of the cultural proficiency continuum and explored culturally responsive practices. In this chapter, you will hone your empathy skills, learn the immense value of vulnerability, and courageously address the topic of privilege. In the process, you'll uncover learning about yourself that you can extend to thoughtfully acknowledge the experiences of others. You will expand your views of what is possible for your students, yourself, and the greater world.

Starting with Empathy

No one wants to sound like an ignorant jerk. My work with professionals from a variety of fields continually proves that cultural proficiency can shield you from this dreaded label. Among the skills that cultural proficiency builds, empathy is one that is getting some well-deserved attention lately. As discussed in Chapter 1, empathy is a crucial leadership skill that promotes deep intellect, problem solving, creativity, social-emotional balance, brain functioning, and productive collaboration. From medical professionals and Fortune 500 leaders to community volunteers and educators, those who practice empathy reap the benefits of its power. Because segregation, faulty curricula, and biased media have yielded a low demand for utilizing empathy, you'll need to access your almighty imagination as a tool in your practice.

 CONNECT AND CONVERSE

> ⟩ Close your eyes and imagine that the world's dominant government leaders and individuals with the greatest wealth and influence are now and historically have been majority Black instead of White. Think about how these various roles and positions would be filled in this world and consider the power and reach they have.

> ⟩ After you have spent some time picturing this as today's reality, consider how White children would be affected by it.

(See **HR8** on p. 82.) [HR]

Embracing Vulnerability and Acknowledging Privilege

The bamboo that bends is stronger than the oak that resists.

—Japanese proverb

Cultural proficiency is not an accomplishment that demands perfection. Embracing this reality converts inevitable awkward missteps into gracefully molded wisdom. Achieving such skillful reactions requires vulnerability. Researcher Brené Brown (2015) teaches that "if we are going to find our way out of shame and back to each other, vulnerability is the path and courage is the light" (p. 110). She underlines this point by asserting that "vulnerability is not weakness; it is our most accurate measurement of courage" (Brown, 2017, p. 154). Seen through this lens, vulnerability in school communities deserves support and praise. My goal in this book is to help you bolster your own courage while you teach others to do the same, creating a model to follow and eventually building a legacy of courage and vulnerability in your school community.

Actively valuing and encouraging vulnerability promises substantial leaps toward empathy and cultural proficiency and sets the stage for learning about an essential yet unpopular topic: privilege. *Privilege* is defined as "a right or immunity granted as a peculiar benefit, advantage, or favor" (*Merriam-Webster*, n.d.). It's a fundamental concept, yet in the context of cultural proficiency, mentions of it are shunned to the extent that laws have been created to decrease the discomfort of those with unearned privileges.

CONNECT AND CONVERSE

> Do you have ample and diverse experience in addressing the concept of privilege?

> If this concept is something you avoid or dislike, what are your reasons?

> Have you observed others' reactions around the topic of privilege? Why do you suppose they react that way?

(See **HR9** on p. 83.) [HR]

One eats while another watches—that is how revolutions begin.

—Turkish proverb

Simply put, formal and informal education systems alike fail to foster the necessary empathy skills to learn about the concept of privilege. Maintaining empathy and grace in both teaching and learning is enriched by acknowledging the reasons why the subject can be so difficult to approach. Doing so will help you eventually normalize this indispensable learning so that everyone benefits. Here are some of these reasons:

- Ignorance and unfamiliarity with the subject matter and other related issues
- Feeling blamed for something one has no control over, including mistakes of ancestors

- Interpreting the concept of privilege as being "spoiled" or "entitled"
- Believing that the hardships one did face are being underestimated
- Responding with defensiveness and denial (often rooted in the learned myth of meritocracy) and refusing to acknowledge desirable outcomes sourced from unearned privileges
- Fearing that privileges will be taken away
- Believing that challenges faced by one marginalized identity are equivalent to those encountered by more severely disenfranchised peoples
- Desiring to remain focused on the identities one is comfortable with, like income level and location, to sidestep topics like racial privilege that may push the shame button

Attempting to avoid the downward pull of shame is a common thread in nearly all these reasons, but the discomfort of wrestling with this topic is nothing compared with the pain that excluded people regularly face on account of ignorance or avoidance. As of 2021, the majority of U.S. public school students identify with disenfranchised identities (National Center for Education Statistics, 2023), and the many I have met have taken notice. What I hear over and over again from students of *all* backgrounds and identities is that they are not only ready but truly eager to learn about privilege: "It's our teachers who are afraid to talk about it." The clear message they, especially those with excluded identities, receive from this omission is that their teachers' discomfort deserves more consideration than their pain. This message obviously takes its toll on prospects for mutually beneficial relationships.

As with cultural blindness (see pp. 48–49 and 63–64), uncomfortable truths can elicit illogical objections. But the undeniable fact is that we *all* have privileges, and the ability to clearly identify them cultivates opportunities for building gratitude, empathy, and knowledge.

Examples of privilege abound. Having access to clean water is one. If this is something you don't think twice about, that's a privilege billions of humans around the world can only dream of (UNESCO, 2023). Your ability to read these words is an outcome of the privileges of literacy and eyesight, the latter of which hundreds of millions of people are deprived of. If you prefer listening to audiobooks, that also involves privileges that are out of reach for countless others, such as optimal hearing health and access to technology. The people who do not have the privileges you do are sure to have their own privileges, but they differ in form, quantity, and quality. Some privileges are more powerful and influential than others. To deny these basic and logical facts perpetuates shame and willful ignorance, which lead to fragility, ingratitude, and insensitivity.

Reversing this downward spiral requires us to face various forms of privilege, including the one most intensely avoided: racial privilege. Historically, racism has relentlessly obstructed equitable access to quality education (Chen, 2015; Du Bois, 1903/1989; Walters, 2001). Educators' unfamiliarity and serious discomfort around subjects like racism and privilege enable this inequity to persist, further emphasizing why it *must* be addressed.

CONNECT AND CONVERSE

> What are your experiences and beliefs around racial privilege?

> Is the topic regularly and openly addressed in your school community? Why or why not?

(See **HR10** on p. 85.) [HR]

Facing the Facts:
Everyone Enjoys Privileges

The satiated do not understand the concern of the hungry.

—Kyrgyz proverb

Expanding your capacity for cultural proficiency requires you to examine everyday examples for how privileges, especially unearned privileges, persevere in shaping worldviews, expectations, experiences, and systems. Again, the moment shame is ignited is the moment you must recall your purpose. Your purpose, your *why*, can empower you to tap into the inestimable strength that lies in your willingness to show courage and vulnerability. Do not allow misdirected shame to interfere with your evolution.

If you identify with marginalized identities, the examples provided in the Privilege Check-In in Figure 4.1 (also available to download at https://www.ascd.org/consciously-unbiased-resources) are not meant to serve as a depressing list of the unwarranted disadvantages you are forced to contend with. My hope is that these examples instead function as evidence of the resilience and strength of disenfranchised peoples who manage to find success in the most challenging circumstances, which is something to be proud of. Further, these are a reminder of people with contrasting identities but similar challenges that you may not have been taught to consider, empathize with, or support.

Finally, whether you have many privileges or just a few, identifying the ones you *do* have empowers you to better utilize them for good. This essential awareness helps you become a stronger advocate for education and justice.

Review, Reflect, Resolve

If you are filled with pride, then you will have no room for wisdom.

—Tanzanian proverb

Review

Figure 4.1 offers an extensive but by no means complete list of privileges as they relate to a number of key social identities. Each privilege listed produces several benefits. Acknowledging these benefits sets you up to be far more successful in creating equitable and inclusive solutions when prompted. To sharpen your empathy skills, please consider to whom the statements apply: insert an X or a check in the M column where it applies to *me;* in the F column for *friends and family;* and in the *S* column for *students.* A statement may apply to more than one of these. Resisting the urge to rush through the list will refine your ability to think beyond the basics. When considering yourself and your family, it's important to practice unadulterated honesty and vulnerability to get the most out of this exercise. When you are unsure of the answer as it relates to others, go with your best guess for now. To build and maintain your practice of thoughtfulness and inclusivity, be sure to consider *all* your students. If even one of your students would be unable to check a box confirming that they hold a given privilege, then you should leave the *S* column unchecked.

Figure 4.1.   Privilege Check-In

Family, Childhood, Education, and Socioeconomic Status	M	F	S
There were more than 20 books and/or plentiful other learning resources in the home I grew up in.			
My parent(s) or caregiver(s) were never unemployed or laid off.			
I have never experienced homelessness.			
My family never had to move because we could not afford the rent or mortgage payment.			
My family owned the house I grew up in.			
I have inherited money or property.			
I never had to skip a meal or suffered long periods of hunger because there was not enough money to buy food.			
I grew up in a relatively safe area where prostitution, drug activity, and high crime rates were not a concern.			
I attended private school or summer camp.			
I have never had to rely primarily on public transportation.			
After graduation, I did not have to be concerned with significant student loan debt.			
Because of my association with a friend or family member, I was offered or had a greater chance for acceptance at a favorable institution or workplace.			
Due to my financial status, I didn't regularly feel ashamed or embarrassed of my substandard clothing, home, method of transportation, etc.			

Family, Childhood, Education, and Socioeconomic Status	M	F	S
Both of my parents attained a college degree.			
I was encouraged to attend college by my parents.			
I had the opportunity to attain a college education.			
I was raised in a two-parent household.			
None of my family members struggled with addiction or a serious mental illness.			
I am not the victim of abuse, nor have I personally witnessed the abuse of loved ones.			
If I choose to learn about my ancestral history, including that of my family's names, that information will most likely be accessible.			
If I choose to learn about the cultural traditions of my ancestors, I can access that information.			
Totals: ____/21			

Mental Health Diagnosis, Learning Ability, Physical Ability	M	F	S
I can go to new places without having to worry about being unable to physically move freely throughout the space.			
I can access all types of media and entertainment, including audio, without the need for closed captioning.			
My eyesight does not require me to obtain a trusted driver to take me where I need to go.			
I do not have to worry that a disability or mental health diagnosis may result in absences that could cause me to lose my job.			
I do not need braille or audio readings to access information from written resources.			
I do not have disabilities that require me to request deadline extensions, alternative assignments, or other accommodations.			
People do not feel uncomfortable looking at me due to their learned discomfort around people with disabilities.			
People do not speak to me or treat me like a child or as though I am unintelligible based on their ignorance about disabilities.			
I never have to worry that a mental health diagnosis or disability will be used to invalidate any argument I make.			
I do not have a mental health diagnosis or disability that was or would be a barrier to having, adopting, or maintaining custody of my children.			

(continued)

Figure 4.1.   Privilege Check-In—(*continued*)

Mental Health Diagnosis, Learning Ability, Physical Ability	M	F	S
I never have to fear that important decisions about my life will be made by others who are considered more qualified based on the perception that their mental abilities, psychological makeup, physical abilities, or learning abilities are superior to mine.			
Stories in the mainstream media about people with my mental health diagnosis or disability, if I have any, are mostly told by people who share my mental health diagnosis or disability.			
Totals: ____/12			

Ethnicity, Language	M	F	S
Neither I nor my ancestors were forced to come to the country I live in today.			
People easily know how to pronounce my name and I am never mocked or perceived as a threat because of it.			
Unfamiliarity or negative assumptions around my name do not hold the potential to limit opportunities or advancement (e.g., employment, acceptance).			
General knowledge about my ethnicity is not usually limited to foods and/or belittling stereotypes.			
When I started school, the primary language spoken there was the same as my native or primary home language.			
My parents do not speak with an accent that leaves them vulnerable to ignorance-based, negative beliefs or actions.			
I can fluently speak and communicate in more than one language.			
I am aware of whether my ancestors spoke another language. That language continues to be fluently spoken and highly valued in my family today.			
I can readily find people, media, and school information utilizing my native language or dialect.			
People do not make assumptions about my intelligence based on my language ability.			
I am never told by others not to speak my language or to get out of "their" country.			
I have a deep understanding of my family's ethnic and cultural traditions.			
I can openly practice and teach others about my family's cultural traditions without any concern of others' disapproval or reprimand.			

Ethnicity, Language	M	F	S
If I criticize the government or discuss why I fear its policies and behavior, I need not worry that I will be seen as a cultural outsider.			
My schools and teachers promoted and undeniably held a high regard for multilingualism without considering some languages to have supremacy over others.			
Totals: ____/15			

Race, Religion	M	F	S
There have never been attempts to scientifically or socially eliminate people of my race or religion.			
People do not assume that I am unintelligent or lazy based on my race or religion.			
I can be accepted into a school or take a job with an equal opportunity employer without having to worry that colleagues may suspect I got the job strictly because of my race.			
I can swear, be tardy, or leave an email unanswered without having people attribute my choices to the alleged bad morals, poverty, or illiteracy of my race or religion.			
People do not assume that I am illiterate or unable to speak the common language due to stereotypes about my race or religion.			
Most of my teachers shared my racial identity.			
Most of my teachers shared my religious identity or were at least familiar with it.			
When I was taught about "civilization" or the heritage of the country I reside in, I was shown ways that people of my race or religion made it what it is.			
If I wish, I can easily arrange to be in the company of people of my race or religion most of the time. This includes work, school, and public spaces.			
People do not regularly ask if they can touch my hair or do so without asking.			
Wherever I go, I can easily and widely find blemish coverage or bandages in "nude" or "flesh" color that will match the color of my skin.			
I can wear my natural hairstyles or headcover without concern of being criticized or punished.			
I can openly eat any foods that I like without being concerned that it may confirm a stereotype negatively associated with my race or religion.			

(continued)

Figure 4.1.   Privilege Check-In—(*continued*)

Race, Religion	M	F	S
I do not have to regularly think about negative perceptions about my race or religion and rarely worry that they may make others uncomfortable.			
When a war or crime against humanity occurs in a part of the world where people share my race or religion, it is fairly and extensively reported on, and victims or refugees are widely supported.			
Stories in the mainstream media about people from my racial group or religion are mostly told by people from my racial group or religion.			
I can achieve or excel without being called a credit to my race or religion.			
I can expect to see many students and professors of my race on a college campus.			
I can be pretty sure that if I ask to talk to "the person in charge," I will be facing a person of my race.			
I can go shopping alone most of the time, fairly confident that I will not be followed or harassed.			
I never have to encounter the following fear-based reactions when people see me: clutching a purse or companion, abruptly locking car doors, wrongly and hastily summoning police, exiting a room or crossing to the opposite side of the path, harassment on airplanes and other forms of transportation, etc.			
When I was a child, my friends and classmates' parents never told them they could not be friends with me due to my race or religion.			
Redlining and housing discrimination are not obstacles that I will have to face to reside in resourced, healthy neighborhoods.			
I do not have a relative or close friend who was wrongly incarcerated.			
I never have to think twice about calling the police when trouble occurs.			
I am confident that the police and other authorities are there to protect me.			
I don't have to worry about incarceration unless I commit a very serious crime.			
If I am ever stopped or questioned by the police or transportation security officers, I need not worry that it may be due to biases around my race or religion.			

Race, Religion	M	F	S
If or when I have children of driving age, I will not need to teach them precise language and behaviors to use if approached by the police to improve their chances of safety.			
If or when I have children, I can arrange to protect them most of the time from people who may mistreat them due to their race or religion.			
If I make an error while driving, I am not worried that my race or religion will be blamed.			
If seeking or being served meals, I am provided with a variety of choices that don't conflict with my religious or spiritual beliefs.			
Most of my teachers celebrated the same religious holidays that I did.			
I can expect to receive days off from work for holidays that matter to me.			
If I choose to attend religious congregations, I will not need to ask for time off from school or work to do so.			
I can dress modestly without encountering unsolicited remarks about it or assumptions that I am being forced to do so.			
If I choose to wear a hoodie and/or dark colors, I don't have to worry that I may be perceived as a threat.			
If I choose to dress modestly, I need not be concerned with ridicule, abuse, or laws created to stop me from pursuing education, employment, or athletics; being involved in my child's education; going on field trips with my child; or enjoying public spaces such as parks and beaches.			
I am rarely subjected to people who want to "save me" from my religion.			
My religion is not commonly misinterpreted as promoting violence and terrorism.			
If I clarify misconceptions about my religion, I need not worry that I will be accused of indoctrination.			
Basic knowledge of my religion is understood, respected, and not confused with other identities like nationality, race, or ethnicity.			
Notions about my religion are not widely based on the cultures or actions of any one country.			
A curriculum including basic facts and truthful history about my race or religion is unlikely to incite accusations of indoctrination or "reverse racism." There are no rules or laws created to eliminate access to these facts.			
Totals: _____/44			

(continued)

Figure 4.1.　Privilege Check-In—(*continued*)

Gender, Sexuality	M	F	S
I do not regularly encounter unsolicited comments about my body.			
My personal and family life is never called into question in the context of my career.			
I can become upset at work without people assuming it is my "hormones," "PMS," or a sign that my gender inherently reduces my abilities to be a qualified employee or leader.			
I have never been the victim of sexual harassment, and it rarely occurs to people who share my gender identity.			
I don't need to worry that I will be taken advantage of when buying a car or requesting a service in a male-dominated field.			
If or when married, I will not be expected to change my name, nor will I be questioned or negatively judged if I choose not to.			
People of my gender are less likely to be the victims of abuse from their partners or spouses.			
My sexuality is most commonly understood as being a naturally inherited identity.			
My gender is the majority represented in positions of leadership in government, law enforcement, executive offices in all sorts of organizations, and other highly influential positions.			
My gender identity is not challenged as a result of my sexual orientation.			
Assumptions about my sexual orientation are not made based on my gender identity.			
I can work with students without worry of being accused of sexual misconduct or corruption due to stereotypes about my sexual orientation or gender identity.			
I can use public restrooms without fear of arrest or verbal or physical abuse.			
I can use public facilities such as gym locker rooms and changing rooms without fear or anxiety.			
Totals: _____/14			

Applicable to Several Identities	M	F	S
I can travel to most places I would like to visit without concern that I may be mistreated, attacked, or threatened due to ignorance or hate for any of the identities I hold.			
I can expect that people will believe me when I report a crime.			
I have never been a victim of violence related to any of my marginalized identities.			
My parents *confidently*, without any hesitation, told me that I could be anything that I wanted to be when I grew up.			
I am assured that the health care I receive will not be negatively affected due to systemic and long-standing biases toward any of my identities that are systemically disenfranchised.			
My teachers never made remarks or taught information that was discriminatory or demeaning toward marginalized identities.			
I am not frequently pressured or expected to explain, justify, or teach about my race, religion, sexual orientation, gender identity, gender expression, or abilities to people who don't share my identities.			
I never have to change my appearance, mannerisms, or behavior to avoid being judged or ridiculed based on my race, religion, sexual orientation, gender identity, gender expression, or abilities.			
If I should ever need to move to a new location, I am not worried that my neighbors will not be neutral or pleasant to me because of my race, religion, sexual orientation, gender identity, gender expression, or abilities.			
I don't need to worry that I may be denied employment because of my race, religion, sexual orientation, gender identity, gender expression, or abilities.			
I can look at the mainstream media and easily find people of my race, religion, sexual orientation, gender identity, gender expression, and abilities represented fairly and in a wide range of roles.			
I have never been accused of cheating or lying because of my race, religion, income, or disability.			
I am never asked to speak for all people of my race, religion, sexual orientation, gender identity, gender expression, or abilities.			
I have never been concerned that I was paid less or treated unfairly at work because of my race, religion, sexual orientation, gender identity, gender expression, or abilities.			
The appearance of my financial reliability is not hindered by negative misconceptions about my race, language, or abilities.			
I was never discouraged from academics or jobs because of my race, religion, sexual orientation, gender identity, gender expression, or abilities.			
Totals: ____/16			

CONNECT AND CONVERSE

Reflect

> Are there any privileges that you had not considered before taking this inventory?

> Did some privileges stand out more than others? If so, why?

> How do your responses compare with those that you predicted for your friends? Your students?

> Check in with your emotions and thoughts at this moment. Do your responses show courageous willingness to be vulnerable and honest, or are they more aligned with avoiding shame? Here are some cues to look for:

> — Did you find yourself questioning the validity of the statements provided?

> — Did you reject the assertion that these privileges are not widely enjoyed by people of marginalized identities?

> Did guilt or shame cause you to justify dismissing privileges you do in fact have?

(See **HR11** on p. 88.) HR

Resolve

- Quench your curiosity and confirm whether your hypotheses were correct. Beginning with a few statements you had to guess on regarding your students, go about respectfully finding actual answers (e.g., through carefully moderated classroom discussions or private student questionnaires).

- Continually practice acknowledging and normalizing discussions around the role that privilege plays in beliefs, actions, and outcomes (to be applied with students, colleagues, and any others you encounter, such as students' parents or caregivers, community members, and friends and family).

- Identify and respond to behaviors resulting from unrealized privileges that threaten productive communications and equitable actions in your school community. This can be especially effective when you yourself hold the privilege at hand and advocate for excluded identities receiving similar advantages. It should be clear that you are not trying to *save* anyone. People don't need saving; they need to be seen and heard. Advocacy isn't about what you will do for them but how you will use your privilege to open doors that enable them to do things for themselves. Wrapping your head around this may require tapping into your empathy stores: what would *you* want? Chances are that you, like most people, wouldn't want pity but, rather, equity and justice. In most cases, a good start begins with the privileged among us reminding others of the voices that deserve to be heard and then inviting those voices to the table. The room and your entire community will be better for it.

Those who are born on top of the anthill take a short time to grow tall.

—Ghanaian proverb

Huda's Responses

 HR8:

**Close your eyes and imagine that the world's dominant gov-
ernment leaders and individuals with the greatest wealth
and influence are now and historically have been majority
Black instead of White. Think about how these various roles
and positions would be filled in this world and consider the
power and reach they have. After you have spent some time
picturing this as today's reality, consider how White children would be affected by it.**

Imagining the given scenario as an actual reality was likely
challenging for you, which illustrates just how deeply ingrained
the status quo is for most of us—to the extent that imagining
an alternative feels incredibly arduous. If this scenario were
the current reality, White children would be deprived of a
vital sense of belonging. Their subsequent lower self-esteem
and motivation for success would almost certainly affect their
engagement and behaviors in and out of school. Their quest
for success would be obstructed by stress that no child should
have to endure. The influence of dominant leaders would teach
much of the world to view White children as being less capable
outsiders. Their excluded and misrepresented identities would
cultivate fear- and hate-induced reactions in others, at times
even provoking bodily harm. The amount of energy they would
continuously have to muster to jump over the hurdles set before
them would be physically, mentally, and emotionally exhausting. Opportunities to fulfill their legacy as role models to their
descendants would be distant dreams polluted by unfair realities. To make matters worse, in this scenario, the grass really
would be greener on the other side. Seeing non-White neighbors
strolling along nearby in blissful ignorance would be a boom-
ing reminder that success is reserved for those granted the
unearned paved path.

Merely imagining a status quo that flips the current racial hierarchy on its head can be used to build empathy. Any outcomes of this scenario that you can imagine are the stark reality for your Black, AAPI, and Brown students. You can use this exercise to empathize with the apparent lack of motivation you see among excluded and disenfranchised students, and to see how success might appear far out of reach for them. Gaining this enriched understanding and developing and applying your empathy skills will enable you to replace the common, hasty reaction of victim blaming that many of us were taught with cues to reassess the curriculum, your classroom environment, and the language you use. You will be equipped with more productive responses that help you profoundly connect with, energize, and empower students. This work gradually yields new mindsets and actions that help you build authentic, positive relationships and foster greater student achievement.

 ## HR9:

Do you have ample and diverse experience in addressing the concept of privilege? If this concept is something you avoid or dislike, what are your reasons? Have you observed others' reactions around the topic of privilege? Why do you suppose they react that way?

Identifying your privileges is mandatory for achieving cultural proficiency, but it's a sensitive issue for many. I carefully think out when and how I teach this topic in my own learning programs. Relatively early in my consulting career, I learned the hard way that addressing the concept of privilege requires building background knowledge and empathy skills.

During a whole-group activity I once was facilitating, a couple of teachers grew vocal about their disdain for the idea of privilege. One teacher explained that her experiences as a White woman raised in an underresourced single-parent household created difficulties equal to those faced by Black people in the United States. When some of her colleagues objected, she leaned hard into the myth of meritocracy. She was encouraged by a White male colleague who grew up in a similar environment to hers. He further explained that although he did not encounter gender discrimination, he faced equivalent prejudices around his appearance because of his numerous tattoos. When he made this statement, the female teacher's expression showed she didn't agree, but to retain her sole supporter, she let his assertion pass.

Although these colleagues' experiences were indeed negative and could be used to build a sense of empathy, I explained why they would still be incomparable to the injustices faced by Black, AAPI, and Brown people in the United States. When their colleagues contributed ideas that supported this response, the two resistant teachers interpreted them as an "attack." Unfortunately, the two teachers' objections arose in the last minutes of the workshop, leaving me little time to clarify misunderstandings. At the end of the session, I invited them to discuss the topic further on another day soon, and the participant evaluations showed me whether they would be likely to take me up on this. The male teacher's review indicated some humility and an openness to learning more; the female teacher's review indicated the opposite. A glowing response, it was not.

My mind raced on my drive home that day. I felt frustrated and misunderstood. At the time, I had some perfectionism and people-pleasing tendencies that exacerbated the issue. I became hyperfocused on the single negative evaluation rather than the dozens of positive ones. I reviewed and reflected on what had happened. Eventually, my internal conversation drew out an attitude of genuine appreciation—not just for the positive feedback and participation but also for the angry response. That breakdown in communication sparked a profound breakthrough. The enlightenment that stemmed from retracing my footsteps markedly enriched how I began preparing audiences for learning about the concept of privilege. I attribute to that experience the fact that I have never since had a similar negative response.

HR10:

What are your experiences and beliefs around racial privilege? Is the topic regularly and openly addressed in your school community? Why or why not?

Thankfully, people's resistance to learning around racial privilege thaws as they advance toward cultural proficiency. This was illustrated in a workshop I facilitated a while ago with school leaders. Similar to the work you engaged with in Chapter 3, educators contemplated how social identities shape perceptions and beliefs. They, too, chewed over why some identities carry more weight than others. One participant I'll call Marco described a charged encounter he had with the concerned parent of a Black student. Visibly frustrated, Marco sought the support of his peers, asking, "Why does it always have to be about race?" At this point, I'll note that, with the exception of only a few, the lived experience of everyone in that room was of a White educator raised and living in the United States. The reactions to Marco's question ranged from disapproving shaken heads to nods of agreement to the programmed hush. I praised Marco's vulnerability and courage in speaking his truth and then asked volunteers to share their thoughts. I watched as gazes slowly shifted toward the few educators in the room who were not White.

Cutting through the silence, Joe, one of the two Black administrators in the room, let out a deep sigh. Turning to Joe, I said, "I might know what that sigh is about." I asked him if he would mind if I shared my prediction and told him to jump in at any time to correct me if I was mistaken. With a soft smile, he agreed. Addressing the entire room, I explained that that sigh is a universal expression commonly understood by excluded individuals. Lisa immediately jumped in: "So how are we ever going to learn about other cultures? If they want us to learn about them, they should be the ones to teach us." It was clear that she was unaware of her unearned privilege of holding identities that were widely and positively taught as a matter of course. In fact, her culture and identities governed the way most of us lived and the experiences we encountered. Further, her identities were not commonly perceived as a threat, nor was she regularly expected to justify her actions or inactions owing to negative stereotypes about her racial identity.

Joe responded, "Imagine life without your privilege of being relieved of that daily pressure to teach others. Our education system and media already did that work for you, so it's probably hard to understand. I spend way too much of my equally important time and energy explaining ideas that I am frankly tired of explaining, ones that should already be understood—especially by the leaders educating and serving as role models for our students today." Even beyond carrying out that extra labor, he explained, by providing the knowledge, he runs the risk of encountering disbelief, defensiveness, or even a threat to his career. He continued:

> It feels like I lose no matter what I do. When the moments arise and I calculate that it may cause more harm to speak my truth, I am bound to face energy-consuming stress later. The dialogue will play over and over in my mind. I'll probably regret not taking the risk to speak up if it could mean even a small possibility that educators would gain a better understanding of their students so that they will feel more valued and loved. Then, I compare it with the possibility of eventually losing my job over it, which means they will be further denied exposure to more inclusive representation.

Joe explained that throughout the dilemma, the frustration and sadness caused by the reality of how racism hurts us all continues to chip away at his already battered soul. His narrative was highly familiar to those in the room with excluded identities who encountered similar struggles.

Joe went on to say that because we were a few sessions into the program series, he felt more comfortable responding to

Marco's question. He explained why it is only logical that racial identity is continually at the forefront of a Black person's mind. Regularly encountering negative assumptions, stereotype threat, and the glaring exclusion of people who look like them drives a constant need for prevention, protection, and defense. The Black, AAPI, and Brown participants in the group concurred that this held true for them as well.

Joe's testimony allowed his colleagues to witness the power unleashed by courage and vulnerability. It yielded reflection and learning that extended beyond the workshop and seeped into daily living. When we met for our next session, several people shared, and nearly everyone agreed that their comfort levels and resilience when discussing race continued to improve. Lisa shared her sincere gratitude for Marco and Joe's contributions. She explained how she had unraveled her feelings through deep reflection in the days following the previous session and how the process had helped her immensely. Another administrator professed that she had been in similar instances as the one Marco had shared, and her initial conclusion had matched his. She admitted that race was an identity she had rarely thought about as a White woman. Her reflections after the workshop had helped her push beyond mere data to notice the real-world effects of racism and marginalization. She acknowledged that although she was still working on becoming more comfortable talking about race, she was convinced that it was worth the effort to overcome: "My discomfort is tolerable, making it incomparable to the struggles faced by my students and their families." She choked up as she shared her last statement: "To be honest, I feel pretty guilty about my dismissive reactions to what I now understand were valid concerns from parents. Shame is talking real loud right now, but I am not going to give in. I am going to use it to make me even more determined to have future reactions that are educated and positive." The silent, attentive group broke into enthusiastic applause.

It is imperative that educational leadership programs include worthy, nonnegotiable learning focused on understanding and dismantling racism (Khalifa et al., 2016).

 HR11:

Are there any privileges that you had not considered before taking this inventory? Did some privileges stand out more than others? If so, why? How do your responses compare with those that you predicted for your friends? Your students? Check in with your emotions and thoughts at this moment. Do your responses show courageous willingness to be vulnerable and honest, or are they more aligned with avoiding shame? Did guilt or shame cause you to justify dismissing privileges you do in fact have?

When addressing the subject of privilege, I have witnessed all sorts of reactions. Some common emotions are disbelief, shock, sadness, anger, resentment, and, most of all, shame. Taking this inventory may have resulted in similar emotions for you. To be clear, I don't want you to feel ashamed about feeling ashamed. I *do* want you to use this challenge as an opportunity for productive contemplation and empathy building. If you are feeling overwhelmed, take a moment to decompress. Know that I am proud of you and cheering you on!

You may have had to acknowledge privileges that you have never thought of before. Because we tend to befriend those who share our key identities, it is likely that you and your friends share many of the same privileges. Assuming this is the case, if neither you nor they experience regular setbacks from other important identities, you simply aren't prompted to discuss or even think about them often. The harsh reality faced by others is mostly out of sight, out of mind. This only makes the truth more difficult to comprehend and accept.

But many students in the United States and throughout the world are likely to have far fewer privileges than the majority of U.S. educators. Remaining out of touch with that reality further reinforces systemic oppression. Escalating your ability to acknowledge these truths without reservation, excuses, or victim blaming will yield immeasurable advantages.

5

Clearing the Lens

*Using Your Critical Consciousness
to Address Exclusionary Behaviors*

The one who develops oneself is twice born.

—Argentinian proverb

In Chapter 4, you unflinchingly explored the challenging topic of privilege. In this chapter, you will learn about a closely linked topic— *exclusionary behaviors* (also referred to as *microaggressions*) and their various forms—and learn how you can activate your critical consciousness to take control of your unconscious biases. To practice sharpening your critical consciousness, I lead you through multiple scenarios and exercises using the *3Rs* (review, reflect, resolve) method to examine norms and rules that are commonplace in U.S. schools.

Using the Rearview Mirror: Exclusionary Behaviors May Appear Smaller Than They Actually Are

It is better to prevent than to cure.

—Peruvian proverb

A while back, I was facilitating a workshop with undergraduates, and we had just finished an activity illustrating the unearned privileges principally reserved for White students. Unexpectedly, one Black student I'll call Alex said he had benefited from many of the same privileges as his White counterparts. With faces of all colors unable to hide their surprise, Alex explained: "I am acutely aware of the injustices faced by Black and Brown people, but I happen to be super fortunate. I know that my older relatives would have been on the other side of this discussion, but it just hasn't been my experience." He disclosed that his parents had both achieved a wealthy financial status, which landed him in an affluent community where he had attended an elite private school. Although he had been among the racial minority there, he felt respected and had made many friends. A flood of inquiries and aha moments followed. Alex and his college peers discussed the beneficial outcomes that emerge in a community that supports all its members, highlighting the advantages in education, health, community, and overall resources afforded by privileged financial status.

Alex admitted that although he had been aware of the obstacles faced by Black and Brown people, his unearned privileges had decreased his ability to develop genuine empathy. In fact, he could recall times when he had agreed with those who have privileged racial identities that many of the reasons for the underachievement of Black and Brown people were under their control and, thus, their own fault.

I refer to this as the "Oprah effect": when people use the extraordinary success stories of those who beat nearly impossible odds to argue that meritocracy is the key to advancement for disenfranchised communities. "If Oprah Winfrey can do it, why can't everyone else?" Alex took a thoughtful pause, and his eyes widened a bit before he chuckled and said, "I think that without knowing it, I may have been Oprah at my school." He observed that the knowledge he had gained in this workshop about privilege had helped him in his personal journey.

Of course, Oprah and others like her *shouldn't* remain the exception, and a critical step for making sure they don't is to address the same conclusion Alex had reached. He didn't notice his own lack of empathy not because he didn't care, but for the same reason it doesn't occur to so many of us: when you don't personally face a given set of challenges, imagining what it is like for those who do isn't usually high on your to-do list. This is why explicit learning around privilege is so necessary. Alex and his classmates left the workshop with the intent to cultivate empathy and use their privileges to lift others up.

But the work doesn't end with learning about social identities and acknowledging privilege. A surefire way to set back your progress is to subscribe to the notion that your learning around one social identity automatically applies to everyone who identifies with it. Indeed, there are countless common beliefs and experiences among those with shared identities, but assuming that is *always* the case breeds stereotypes. Such narrow understandings are often revealed through subtle but harmful exclusionary behaviors.

Exclusionary behaviors, or microaggressions, are programmed reflexes and the most prevalent symptom of unconscious biases. When observed in isolation by the unenlightened eye, these actions may appear insignificant and easily dismissible. Like their source of unresolved unconscious biases, exclusionary behaviors often occur discreetly, making them more dangerous. They communicate hostile, derogatory, or ignorant viewpoints and perpetuate notions of supremacy (Sue et al., 2007). If this description of these behaviors sounds very serious, it is. And exclusionary behaviors are one of the most common concerns reported to me from educators and students.

Effects and Categories of Exclusionary Behaviors

It's not the load that kills—it's the excessive load.

—Dominican proverb

The person who attracts mosquitoes can understand that it isn't the one mosquito bite that drives victims to complain, retreat, or, in my case, exhibit sheer madness. The fact that it occurs repeatedly is what does us in. In the case of our college student Alex, his Black racial identity exposed him to some exclusionary behaviors, but because of his sheltered upbringing, his experiences were relatively insignificant compared with those of others with excluded identities who did not have his other privileges. Having numerous privileged identities frequently results in a reduced ability to cultivate empathy and understanding for those who *do* encounter excessive exclusionary behaviors. Fortunately, those who don't personally experience exclusionary behaviors can still attain this skill set, required for cultural proficiency, through learning. Read on.

Those who encounter exclusionary behaviors at school or in the workplace must carry the extra weight of stereotype threat, racial battle fatigue, and a diminished sense of belonging due to an inability to freely be their authentic selves. Once again, use your imagination to tap into your empathy skills. Envision that your racial identity is one that is commonly stereotyped as being "lazy." In this scenario, you have encountered this stereotypical belief before and know the outcome threatens your well-being and livelihood. At work, you are going to do all you can to ensure none of your actions reinforce this stereotype. You are considering not only how you are impacted by this belief but also how your individual actions will reinforce this stereotype and its imposition on your entire racial group. Continually trying to disprove this stereotype is adding so much more stress to your life that you do not need. Your colleagues of a dominant racial identity do not need to worry about this stereotype threat. If they reply late to an email, miss a deadline, or move a bit slower on a long day, their coworkers, supervisors, and clients will draw conclusions based on who they are as individuals, without considering their race as a factor.

This example demonstrates the importance of providing broad exposure to diverse identities and to diversity within those identities. Those missing windows, mirrors, and sliding doors compounded with exclusionary behaviors produce *imposter syndrome,* which often crops up when individuals overcome obstacles to achieve out-of-the-box success but feel undeserving of their accomplishments. Effects include internalized feelings of inadequacy that constrain motivation in even the strongest characters and plant the seeds of self-doubt about their strengths, actions, and ability to achieve real success

(Martin, 2018). Thus, in our scenario, even if you are an outstanding performer, it is likely you are afflicted with imposter syndrome and feel disengaged and isolated, while your potential for advancement and greater contribution to your school or workplace dwindles.

The scenario you just imagined is the harsh reality for students and educators with excluded identities. The effects of race-related exclusionary behaviors also contribute to *racial battle fatigue*—a result of repeated exposure to exclusionary behaviors that has damaging effects on emotional, mental, and physical health. Research (Geronimus et al., 2006) shows that Black women in particular have deteriorated health owing to repeated encounters with bias. This stress is further exacerbated by sexual harassment, another effect of bias that is unfortunately widespread in academia (National Academies of Sciences, Engineering, and Medicine, 2018).

The collective effects of bias and the resulting exclusionary behaviors have the power to spoil major life decisions and aspirations. Remedies include culturally proficient practices that provide ample "mirrors, windows, and sliding doors." Just as important, you must become adept at identifying, preventing, and appropriately responding to exclusionary behaviors. Exclusionary behaviors can be broken down into several categories, which I define on the following pages (Sue et al., 2007).

Calling the police due to suspicions of a Black or Brown individual in the vicinity

Using derogatory terms to describe a female leader

Refusing to rent a property or sell an item to someone with a marginalized identity

Spreading inflammatory propaganda (e.g., from biased and unfair news reports)

BLATANTLY BIASED BEHAVIORS,

also called **microassaults**, are the most obvious exclusionary behaviors. They are intentional, made with the awareness that they may be hurtful.

Making negative remarks about religious or cultural dress

Making a racist or transphobic joke

10 EXAMPLES

Knowingly scheduling a due date or an exam on a cultural or religious holiday

Telling someone Brown or of AAPI heritage to "go back to your own country"

Making sweeping negative stereotypes about marginalized groups, like "All Muslims are terrorists" or "Women are too emotional to be good leaders"

Responding to testimonies of discrimination faced by those with marginalized identities by saying that "if they don't like it, they can leave"

Using male pronouns to refer to people of all genders

Saying, "You don't look/sound/act like [any nondominant ethnicity]."

Mistaking a Black, AAPI, or Brown administrator for a service or support staff member

Telling a woman dressed in hijab that she should dress "more modern" because she is "in America now"

Mistaking a female doctor for a nurse

EXCLUSIONARY INSULTS
are less obvious than blatantly biased behaviors, yet sometimes equally harmful. Exclusionary insults can occur regularly in virtually all settings.

Staring at a woman's body rather than her face

10 EXAMPLES

Asking Brown people or people of AAPI heritage (but not White people) where they are "really from"

Praising Black, AAPI, or Brown people for their "excellent English"

Assuming that students with disabilities should be primarily in life skills programs or not considering them for advanced academic programs

Raising your voice when addressing someone who is blind or whose first language is not English

Source: Used with permission of Huda Essa. © 2024 Huda Essa.

Calling oneself "color-blind"

Showing a preference for "equal" rather than "equitable" practices

Labeling equitable opportunity initiatives or learning around cultural proficiency as racist against White people

Responding to measures like the Equal Opportunity Employment Act by saying, "I just think the most qualified person should get the position."

EXCLUSIONARY INVALIDATIONS
are actions and words that deny the experience of people in marginalized groups.

Denying the existence of xenophobia and various "isms"

Referring to severe injustices and oppression as "ancient history"

10 EXAMPLES

Being unwilling to learn how to pronounce an unfamiliar name

Regularly asking unmarried or childless employees to do additional tasks or work later than others

Telling people with marginalized identities that they "are too sensitive" or "don't know how to take a joke" when they are hurt or offended by a derogatory comment

Not speaking directly to a person with a disability or who speaks English with an accent

Depending on context, exclusionary behaviors may sometimes fall under more than one category. The objective of these definitions and examples is not to provide precise instances to measure your experience against but, rather, to enhance your ability to identify a variety of exclusionary behaviors. Pay attention, and you'll observe how they have the potential to show up anywhere, in professional and social spaces alike. The mosquitoes are relentless.

 CONNECT AND CONVERSE

> Have you encountered any exclusionary behaviors yourself? If so, are they regular or occasional occurrences?

— If you do not encounter exclusionary behaviors frequently, imagine what it would be like if you did have to deal with this added stress. Choose one of your identities, think of a negative misconception related to it that you might encounter, and imagine exclusionary behaviors that could stem from that ignorance.

> What is your reaction to exclusionary behaviors when they occur? If you rarely encounter exclusionary behaviors and had to imagine some for the previous prompt, how do you think you would react if you encountered them 10 times? 100 times? Do you think your reaction to the 10th insulting exclusionary behavior would be the same for the 100th?

> Which exclusionary behaviors from the examples provided on pages 95–97 stood out to you? Were they ones you've faced? Ones that you yourself have committed? Ones you've witnessed, not knowing they were harmful? Consider the response of the targeted individual(s) and reflect on why they may have had the reaction they had.

(See **HR12** on p. 123.) [HR]

Effectively Responding to Exclusionary Behaviors

The ignorant are their own enemy.

—Palestinian proverb

One of the chief concerns students share with me, apart from exclusionary behaviors coming from their teachers, is their teachers' failure to address exclusionary behaviors that occur among students. Like educators' avoidance of the topic of privilege, the programmed hush around exclusionary behaviors is observed by students, who receive the same message from that silence: their teachers' comfort overrules their well-being.

Interrupting exclusionary behaviors and responding to them appropriately is nonnegotiable. This rule applies to what spills out of your mouth *and* the mouths of others. Effective interventions and responses to exclusionary behaviors include acknowledging the experiences and any silence or discomfort around them. A humble confession of the challenges they pose for you models courageous vulnerability and will foster trust and mutually respectful relationships with and among students. It's important to practice this with colleagues and caregivers, too.

Perfection is not required. We are all bearing witness to our rapidly changing world, and every scenario occurs within a context and culture and among a specific population and set of circumstances that no manual could address with exactitude. Therefore, like nearly all lessons in becoming culturally proficient (and the reason my goal for you is to evolve into your own manual), there is no precise best answer to every exclusionary behavior. Still, although I can't offer a specific response or script, keep in mind that your main objectives are to support the targets of exclusionary behaviors and foster learning to prevent similar exclusionary behaviors from occurring (or reoccurring). In addition, the following guidelines could benefit any situation:

- Remain focused on the idea or belief that the exclusionary behavior stems from, rather than the person demonstrating the behavior.
- Question the validity and logic of the exclusionary behavior.
- Acknowledge the intent, especially when it appears to be positive, but concentrate on the impact.
- Share any prior knowledge you have that may increase understanding of the idea or belief the exclusionary behavior stems from. Examples of background knowledge you could tap into include the history behind the idea, how it relates to injustices faced by other identities, unwanted outcomes, and so on.
- Increase the perpetrator's empathy skills by reframing the issue in a way that relates to their identities or the identities of others of significance (e.g., classmates, family, other loved ones).
- Validate the targeted individual's feelings and experience.
- Uphold the current priority, which is the safety and well-being of the targeted individual. Base your next steps on what you know about them and what you observe about their current state. If you are unsure, pull them aside for a quick check-in, saying, "I am sorry that this happened to you. It is important that the class learn from this so that the mistake is not repeated. I will teach the lesson, but I want you to decide whether you'd like me to do that now or if you prefer that I address it later." Their input will help you decide whether you will move forward with the teachable moment or keep your point concise for now. If you save the lesson for later, this doesn't mean that you are dropping it but that you will gather more information, regroup, and address it again in the near future in a more thoughtful manner. You can apply a similar approach to other scenarios where you don't yet feel prepared to knowledgeably address the situation. It is important that you share your reasoning and plan with the targeted individual.
- If the targeted individual agrees to move forward with the class's deeper processing of the event, allow space for them to respond, but refrain from making a pointed request.

- For this open discussion to be as productive and meaningful as possible, other students willing to volunteer should be invited into the discussion as well. Their input could further increase empathy skills, resolve related conflicts, promote the kind of mindfulness that prevents the exclusionary behavior from reoccurring, and increase the overall level of community and respect in your classroom.
- Applaud the courageous vulnerability of all involved.
- Set and share your high expectations for improved communications and empathy moving forward.

As you read these guidelines, you might notice that they relate to concepts you have already learned. I am pointing this out because I want you to recognize that you already have what it takes to support your students with confidence. Remember that exclusionary behaviors mostly stem from unresolved unconscious biases that were imposed on us without question. Therefore, aggressors often underestimate the impact of their actions. Be empathetic when addressing the perpetrator of an exclusionary behavior, whose response might show anything from surprise and embarrassment to sheer apathy. Being careful that the aggressor doesn't feel attacked does not enable their aggression but, rather, helps you curb hostility they or others may feel. Maintaining a thoughtful and calm approach yields a productive learning experience for everyone.

When it is you who carries out an exclusionary behavior, acknowledge that this is just another shuffle in your dance from unlearning to learning. Although some of this conversation may occur internally as you reflect, it is important that you share your conclusions and apologize for the effect of your words or actions. Eventually, your ability to foster inclusive practices will prevent many exclusionary behaviors from occurring and causing damage in the first place.

Moments of Surprise Are Glimmers of Gold: Activating Your Critical Consciousness

If you take big paces, you leave big spaces.

—Burmese proverb

As you steadily move toward cultural proficiency, regularly activating your *critical consciousness* will offer you a turbo boost. If you're unfamiliar with this term, think of it as a filter to help you process information before it solidifies into your beliefs. It is the ultimate tool for taking control of your unconscious biases.

On my own journey, I discovered that one of the easiest and most valuable ways to activate my critical consciousness was merely to notice my "moments of surprise." This is how I define those fleeting real-world instances that make our unconscious biases visible and show that we have some unlearning to do. Many who have learned this strategy at my workshops have come to the same conclusion: moments of surprise serve as golden opportunities not to be missed.

To illustrate, let's revisit the vignette from the beginning of Chapter 2, where I described my colleague's response to her new class roster. This teacher became upset when she read the labels assigned to her students. With the knowledge that we've gained, we can now see that her reaction revealed the biases she held around the labels. Let's move a step further now to consider what might have happened when she eventually met her students. That meeting would present this teacher's potential moment of surprise—a moment that presents itself as a result of her inaccurate assumptions about students' language ability, appearance, comprehension levels, or home life. Similar occurrences arise when we meet colleagues, caregivers, and others whose names we see in an email before meeting them in person. The moments of surprise that contradict negative assumptions can continue to manifest throughout the school year. Unfortunately, unless you are open to noticing these moments when they occur, even the most contested biases are likely to persist. But if we are intent on remaining observant, we will gain knowledge and wisdom, empowering us to know and do better in the future.

Reviewing and reflecting on moments of surprise are key to honing your critical consciousness skills. You must pay close attention to instances that invalidate your restrictive preconceived notions. Otherwise, you leave the door wide open for achievement-withering confirmation bias to rule. *Confirmation bias* is the tendency to look for information that supports, rather than rejects, one's preconceptions, typically by interpreting evidence to confirm existing beliefs while rejecting or ignoring any conflicting data (APA, n.d.). For instance, believing that certain families are less involved in their child's schooling makes you more likely to recall instances that support that bias rather than ones that disprove it. This is a weak spot for most of us. It generally feels good to be right, and confirmation biases are fueled by that desire. Allowing such biases to flourish unchecked results in negative cycles like the unconscious bias cycle in Figure 2.1 (p. 31). Having a lack of awareness around your biases maintains flawed assumptions that fuel lower expectations, exacerbating the under-achievement of school communities. The courageous educator seeks factual knowledge, truth, and justice over fleeting, misleading beliefs. You are that courageous educator. Your heightened awareness around confirmation biases and moments of surprise is vital to interrupting destructive cycles.

Using the 3Rs Method

So once you have noticed the moment of surprise or caught yourself almost yielding to confirmation biases, what's next? You will be sharpening your critical consciousness skills using a simple strategy that you have already been practicing at the end of each chapter: the 3Rs method. I created this method as an accessible three-step (*review, reflect, resolve*) process to ignite the knowledge and empathy needed to reform education and, by extension, improve our world. Although this approach is simple and can be used anywhere, it compels you to seek and compile evidence to ensure thoughtful, educated beliefs and actions. When this approach is used regularly and thoroughly, the need for its use diminishes as it generates natural automaticity and increased self-confidence. It frees you to engage more fully in conversations and actions, demolishing worries that disrupt growth and true diversification. The method can be used in and applied to an unending number of experiences and environments, all gliding you further along on your journey. I now want you to learn how to access the method independently. Let's start by looking at a real-world example:

> Jada is standing in line at the grocery store. In front of her stands a woman who appears to be of Asian descent. As the woman unloads her cart, she glances at Jada, who smiles and says hello. Without making a response, the woman quickly turns back to the task at hand. Jada feels slightly offended and thinks this is very rude. She then brushes it off with what qualifies as confirmation bias of a stereotype: the woman is Asian, so not making eye contact or showing warmth is in her culture.

This fleeting moment offers a gold mine of opportunity for deep evaluation and authentic growth. Once again, you'll be practicing your empathy skills by putting yourself in Jada's position as you walk through this scenario. Although you might not have experienced Jada's exact interaction and thought process, her bias is comparable to biases formed around an immense number of identities. This example can serve as a resource for you to return to for reflection when subsequent such occasions arise. The following breakdown of the 3Rs method demonstrates how Jada could use the moment to activate and strengthen her critical consciousness. Each step illustrates how the 3Rs can fast-track your journey through the process of learning, unlearning, and diversification.

The first *R* stands for **Review**. Review the bias. Notice the assumptions made. In this case, the assumption is that Asian cultures do not promote warmth, communication, or eye contact.

The second *R* stands for **Reflect**. Reflections may occur in a finite period and are likely to arise repeatedly and evolve over time. After identifying the bias, reflect on its origin and outcomes. In this example, here are some questions worthy of consideration:

- Do you communicate regularly with many Asian individuals?
- If so, does your experience include Asian people from diverse backgrounds and locations?
- In what *context* do you normally interact with Asian people?
- Do those contexts allow for a broad range of communications, or only select types of communications?
- How might your role in the interaction have influenced each party's behaviors, emotions, and outcomes?
- If your communications with Asian people are primarily through your role as an educator, how might the dynamics of authority/educator to student or caregiver influence those experiences and outcomes?
- How might communications differ if the context were altered?
- Can you identify which privileges carry influence around the bias held?
- Would you have attributed the woman's behavior to her culture if she had been White?
- If the woman had been White, would you be more likely to assume that her behavior resulted from distinct experiences and individual character traits rather than presume notions about her culture or her race?
- Can you see how identities with wide representation are granted diverse reasoning and excuses for their actions?
- Giving consideration to this woman's individuality, what reasons, outside her race, may have influenced her reaction?
- If people form a negative or underinformed judgment about one of your actions, how would you prefer they respond to it?

This seemingly simple occurrence offers learning opportunities Jada (and you) can use to improve countless future experiences. Asians currently account for more than half of the human population. Jada's initial unconscious bias was an impulsive thought that was formed by a broad stroke of a single paintbrush over a massive, extremely diverse population. Now, you may meet Asian people who say that in their case, the bias is not far from the truth. But this doesn't mean the bias applies to all people of that identity. Reviewing and reflecting on the bias helps you to create space for rightfully honoring individuality. It strengthens your critical consciousness to the point that you can do the necessary unlearning—and then go on to prevent future formation of similar biases. A bonus is that the confirmation biases you do go on to create will be focused on the common good that can be found among people. That healthy dose of optimism benefits educators and students alike.

The final *R* stands for **Resolve**. This step steers your resolution toward being the ancestor or inspirational leader that uses wisdom to create change. Here, you decide how you will share your discoveries to foster empathy and advocacy that resound beyond this isolated experience to inspire thoughtful and inclusive practices for countless humans today and tomorrow.

Resolutions rarely fit within a prescribed time frame. Some may be immediate, whereas others unfold over several years, whenever opportunities to put the learning into action present themselves. The following are some sample initial resolutions that one may generate through the 3*R*s process. These could be applied to a plethora of scenarios you might encounter yourself.

- Remain vigilant of confirmation biases and reflexive stereotypes when they appear and immediately replace them with sound reasoning that credits individuality. Do this until it becomes your instinctive response.
- Use a "maybe" association when predicting reasons for people's actions or beliefs (e.g., "*Maybe* she wasn't actually looking at me but something near me" or "*Maybe* she is just having a rough day"). The point is to recognize that reasoning can be as diverse as humans are.
- Educate yourself more on the topic at hand and others associated with it.

- Gain further insight through informal relationships and communications with people who share the identity you've been reflecting on.
- Expand learning opportunities through literature and media that illustrate the immeasurable diversity of that identity.
- Seek the common threads that build empathy as it relates to you personally as well as to significant others, including members of your school community.
- Share your wisdom with others. To make that sharing most meaningful, you may relate your experience to...
  - Stereotypes or similar narratives shared with you from family, ancestral history, friends, colleagues, and students.
  - Recognition of how biases and their outcomes promote the idea that various identities have supremacy.
  - Ways in which exclusion, misrepresentation, and the resulting biases hurt us all.

I am excited for you to continue using the 3Rs in various areas of your life and regularly applying them to your professional practice. I included the scenario with Jada purposely as an example of how using the 3Rs method with an occurrence outside the school community can boost your cultural proficiency and make you a stronger educator.

For the remainder of this chapter, I provide further opportunities for you to use the 3Rs in the context of your school community. Because culture is everything, we'll start there. Let's set the scene by revisiting the subject of cultural norms.

CONNECT AND CONVERSE

Select a cultural norm you've witnessed that differs from your own. If you can think of one from any of your students' cultures, choose one of those.

> How did you learn about this norm?

> How does the norm differ from your own?

> ⟩ Has your knowledge of this norm shaped any of your communications or practices?

(See **HR13** on p. 125.) HR

3*R*s Example: The "No Interruptions" Rule

You can't wake a person who is pretending to be asleep.

—Navajo proverb

Exercising your critical consciousness through the 3*R*s will help you learn effectively from your observations. This applies not just to the norms adhered to by others but also to those you abide by yourself. Attaining cultural proficiency requires you to review and reflect on the norms you follow to assess whether they are truly equitable and inclusive. Only then can your resulting resolutions help you improve.

Review

Let's zoom in on a common norm, or rule, in U.S. schools: the one that tells students not to interrupt. At first glance, it appears to help maintain order and peace in the classroom. It seems simple enough, yet this rule is regularly broken, resulting in interruptions that take learners off task. Subsequent disciplinary measures may include removing students from instructional time altogether.

Reflect

The second *R* prompts deeper reflection that takes us to eye-opening revelations. Like many others, the no-interruptions rule is rarely questioned because it appears to make perfect sense. But when implemented without due diligence and reflection, it can reflect cultural destructiveness.

Wait! Before you throw this book at the wall, hear me out. What might be "common sense" to you is not common to everyone. Like unconscious biases, rules and norms that have long been in place are not questioned, but they should be. Questioning these norms reveals that many of them repress learning for students unaccustomed to practicing them in the additional cultures they identify with. Further, refusing to investigate a norm's effectiveness demonstrates a belief in the supremacy of the dominant culture. I don't know about you, but in my family, and with many of my Black and Brown friends, we don't always "wait our turn" when we have something to say. Many cultures include norms accepting of the idea that if someone else is speaking at length, it is not rude to interrupt. The perspective is that "interrupting" is merely a way of contributing to the conversation when a relevant thought arises.

I urge you to practice empathy here and recall similar situations you have been in. Can you remember a time when you had a thought to share but didn't want to interrupt the person speaking, and by the time they finished, you had forgotten what you wanted to say, or the focus of conversation had changed entirely? In the end, the conversation's potential was limited by your inability to contribute your ideas or share timely support for the speaker's ideas.

Like most norms, this one stems from larger cultural norms. A culture that places a high value on collectivism may be more likely to validate "interruptions" and consider them an aspect of active listening. A collectivist culture also invites more vocal support for the speaker that is directed toward the statement listeners are responding to precisely when it occurs. A "yes!", an "amen!", or any other positive acknowledgment can do wonders for social connectedness within a group. It fosters a sense of belonging, which increases motivation and engagement and expands the group's potential for success.

On the other hand, you can see how this style of dialogue may require more time, a resource most teachers aren't swimming in. This norm could also prevent the original speaker from completing their thought if time runs out or they lose their train of thought after someone jumps in. Also, you may have students whose norms outside school match the ones they follow in school, and those deserve similar consideration.

Resolve

We now arrive at the third *R*, where we develop reflections into resolutions. Managing differences in a way that benefits everyone is not just possible but also an excellent opportunity to model treating diversity as the incredible asset that it is. The following resolutions are organized in a sample step-by-step process that you can apply to this scenario and then later to others:

- Explain to students the importance of learning from different cultures and communication styles.
- Get to know your students. Respectfully inquire about the norms they adhere to, in this case focusing on conversation styles. You are sure to find commonalities and differences among their various cultures. Variables include modifications and adaptations of behaviors and beliefs according to context, environment, speaker identities such as authority figures and elders, and so on.
- Identify and honor the assets of various cultural norms (including respectfully listening and engaging, giving timely responses, providing feedback and additional ideas, and offering encouragement and support).
- Invite students into the brainstorming process for creating a new norm related to class discussion. When allowed to do so, students often have the most creative solutions to share. They are much more likely to adhere to a rule they helped create because they have a greater sense of inclusion, ownership, and respect than when they are simply given a rule to follow. This sort of collaboration is an example of cultural responsiveness that follows a norm aligned with collectivist cultures.
  - As teacher, your objective is to collectively create classroom norms that allow for optimal learning opportunities that are culturally proficient rather than culturally destructive. Record feedback of the various perspectives and discuss the benefits and obstacles to be considered for each suggestion. The goal is a successful, cooperative learning environment.

In my personal experience, the process took about 15 minutes but saved me hours of time and energy in the long run!

Here are some ideas from my own classroom teaching days. Most of these actually come from my former 3rd grade students:

- Teach students intercultural communication skills that help them identify appropriateness based on context and audience. Students with these vital life skills experience greater success because they can pick up on and respect norms in a variety of environments (e.g., professional settings, other classrooms, new cultural settings).
- Designate which lessons or dialogues allow for which type of communication style.
  - Students agreed that "interrupting" or "adding on" would be best applied in small-group work or certain whole-group activities allowing for shouted out responses. Some students even suggested additional criteria: the information must be helpful, encouraging, thought-provoking, or questioning. They added the rule that even when interrupted, the speaker must be given the opportunity to eventually complete their thought.
  - In lessons where interrupting sets back learning, students would actively participate without "adding on" until the speaker is finished. They would accomplish this by taking note of anything they wanted to contribute and then sharing once the speaker completed their thought.
  - There would also be more defined expression outlets, such as taking turns in a think-pair-share or small-group work, where after each idea is shared, the rest of the group is given the opportunity to respond, ask questions, add on, or offer encouragement.
  - Interrupting is highly encouraged when disrupting hate speech, harassment, or bullying.

- Nonverbal signs of support like snapping fingers or golf claps are always welcome.

- Provide alternative outlets to release verbal energy, such as recess and short breaks.
- Encourage students to use additional means to communicate with classmates and their teacher, such as writing letters. (I used an empty shoebox to create a mailbox at my desk. Students had the idea of using their personal storage shelves for receiving letters.)

This scenario illustrates how exercising your critical consciousness strengthens your ability to provide authentic, inclusive, and culturally responsive instruction. And in turn, students gained valuable cooperative learning skills and increased their engagement and sense of community.

3*R*s Example: The "English Only" Rule

Let's move through the 3*R*s again, using a different scenario. This one is written in the second person, with the aim of eliciting deeper meaning and empathy.

Review

As they walk into class, a few of your Emergent Multilingual Learners are speaking to one another in Haitian Creole. They begin laughing and then look over at you. One of their classmates who, like you, doesn't know Haitian Creole appears annoyed. Frustration kicks in because you have already reminded them of the "English only" rule several times today. This instance confirms your reason for why this rule is in place.

The look on your face leads the students to frantically explain themselves, but by now, you are fed up with the excuses. Their actions are insubordinate and do not deserve one more minute of the class's time. You tell them again that they can speak their native language outside school, but in your classroom, they should speak only English.

You reiterate that this is so that their English will improve. You record their misbehavior. Because this is a repeat offense, school rules indicate that they must report to the principal's office, and their caregivers will be notified. Your principal also does not tolerate such behaviors, which makes it easier to follow through without question.

Reflect

After you review the incident in your classroom, reflect on the following questions:

- What are your expectations for the short- and long-term success of your Emergent Multilingual Learners?
- What are the origins of your beliefs? Are they based on significant scholarly research, or are they ideas you've absorbed over the years without question?
- When and for whom is bilingualism considered an asset?
- Which languages appear to be more desirable and acceptable than others?
- Do you value various dialects as distinct languages that hold assets from the adjacent culture (e.g., languages influenced by bicultural identities, such as African American Vernacular English and Spanglish)?
- What is the extent of your knowledge of inequities encountered by Emergent Multilingual Learners and their families?
- Do you have significant evidence that your instruction and classroom practices effectively support language learning for all students?
- Do the families of your Emergent Multilingual Learners receive equitable support and unbiased, inclusive interactions that encourage their involvement in the school, in turn increasing their children's engagement and achievement?
- Do you hold evidence that your classroom environment honors a variety of languages and cultures?
- Do your school's or classroom's policies affect other students' actions and beliefs around Emergent Multilingual Learners and the additional languages they speak?

- Is it possible that your students weren't saying anything offensive but merely joking around?
- Do you generally let students make inoffensive jokes in class?
- Do you commonly assume that people speaking another language around you are saying something offensive or troublesome? If so, could your own unconscious bias have produced xenophobic beliefs and behaviors?
- How can confirmation bias present itself in scenarios like this one?
- Why do these actions model cultural destructiveness and reinforce negative unconscious biases for your students?
- How can the actions taken produce diminished self-esteem, decreased academic achievement, damaged student-teacher relationships, and further discrimination from students who will follow your lead?
- How do the numerous outcomes of the disciplinary actions—including students' missing instructional time and the potential harm done to the school's relationships with their families—contribute to visibly devaluing multilingualism and maintaining the status quo?

Resolve

After the reflection stage, you will probably realize there is much to learn, so your main resolution will be to educate yourself. The following resolutions fall under that umbrella:

- Learn about the deep history of xenophobia that led to culturally destructive practices such as the elimination of native languages. In the United States, nearly all families or their ancestors encountered this culturally destructive practice, including (but not limited to) Italian, Irish, Polish, Vietnamese, Japanese, Russian, and German immigrants—the list goes on and on. Countless people succumbed to the repression of their native language. Other groups, such as the Indigenous and enslaved peoples, were literally forced to do so. As a result of this repression, you may now be dispossessed of the ability to speak your family's native language. The more you learn about these histories from people you meet, the more you will witness how widespread this was and, regrettably, still is today.

- Consider the many disadvantages language suppression and the consequent loss of other cultural assets create for individuals and how they eventually translate into losses for entire communities, nations, and the world.
- Acknowledge that our brains are wired to be multilingual (Phillips & Pylkkänen, 2021). Humans are highly capable of learning new languages and speaking multiple languages. In fact, students around the world do this with ease every day. Many countries value learning more than one language and certainly enjoy the benefits.
- Recognize that there is no evidence that continuing to speak one's native language will inhibit one's ability to learn a new language. In fact, data shows that students' use of their native languages increases their proficiency in the new language they are learning, and bilingual and multilingual students' mastery of their native language is tied directly to their school readiness and success (Zelasko & Antunez, 2000).
- Realize that multilingualism allows for regular movement between two or more languages, igniting brain activity and flexibility, which enhances cognitive development (U.S. Department of Education, 2015). When compared with monolingual peers, multilingualism supports students' abilities to more easily
  - Form and access strong metalinguistic skills.
  - Use flexible thinking skills, including higher levels of logic and abstract thought.
  - Solve word problems and math concepts.
  - Focus, recall information, and make decisions.
  - Learn additional languages.
  - Resist the distraction of irrelevant information.
  - Access wider-ranging background knowledge that enriches and advances new learning.

- Maintain strong ties with their culture, community, and family.
- Use their languages to create even more relationships.
- More diversely participate in and learn from the global community.
- Attain advanced levels of cultural competence and empathy because language is deeply embedded in culture and vice versa.
- Attain skills that improve employment opportunities.

- Learn what research has to say about dual language education. Longitudinal research finds that dual language enrichment models of schooling, in which students' learning mostly occurs using two languages throughout the school day, enhance student outcomes and contribute to closing the academic potential gap in students' second language (Collier & Thomas, 2004):
  - On standardized assessments, bilingual students in effective dual language programs meet or exceed the performance of their English-only peers.
  - Dual language schooling increases the potential for a more inclusive and supportive school community for teachers, administrators, students, and their parents or caregivers.
  - Learning more than one language is not only beneficial to Emergent Multilingual Learners but also to monolingual English speakers, who can benefit greatly from learning another language without any loss to learning. It will only enhance their achievement and outcomes.

- Take inventory of cues and evidence that indicate whether your school community effectively supports your Emergent Multilingual Learner community. Be sure to include and value various dialects of English (e.g., African American Vernacular English, Hispanic American Vernacular English, Appalachian English,

Southern American English) as well as other forms of cross-cultural English varieties (e.g., Spanglish, Banglish, Arabeezi). In the United States and throughout the world, languages and dialects endlessly grow and evolve. Each language brings priceless assets and an enhanced ability to connect and communicate with more people in more places. An English-only policy makes it difficult for a school to meet the needs of Emergent Multilingual Learners. As Hollie (2017) observes, "The needs of students who use unaccepted languages have been ill served by educational policies that have contributed to institutionalized linguistic prejudice" (p. 180).

- Foster a classroom environment that not only encourages multilingualism but promotes it for *all* students.
- Model learning from various languages in your classroom and inspire your students and colleagues to do the same.
- Be a stronger advocate for providing inclusive and equitable practices that better involve, inform, and empower multilingual families.

I hope moving through this 3*Rs* example further confirms the power you can harness from your critical consciousness skills to be a more powerful advocate and leader.

 CONNECT AND CONVERSE

> Can you speak more than one language?

> Do you speak the additional language your ancestors spoke? Why or why not?

> Did your caregivers encourage you to learn or speak another language?

> Do you wish you could speak an additional language?

(See **HR14** on p. 128.) HR

3*R*s Example: Your Turn to Reexamine Common Norms and Rules

*To learn a language is to have one more
window from which to look at the world.*

—Chinese proverb

It's your turn now! Use the following prompts to guide your 3*R*s practice around norms you carefully observe in your school community.

Review

School and classroom routines, rules, and procedures are all dictated by norms from one or more cultures. Assess the inclusiveness (and therefore effectiveness) of the following list of common school and classroom rules, routines, and norms and consider which larger cultural norms they are dictated by. Examine your own school and classroom rules through this lens.

- Students enter the school building and their classrooms in a quiet and orderly manner.
- Students engage in start-of-class and dismissal routines without distraction.
- Students use good manners and polite language to address school staff.
- Students do not use personal tech devices during class.
- Students do not use obscenity (as defined by teachers and administration).
- Students walk, don't run, in single file in the hallway and during transitions.
- Students follow school rules about which clothing and hairstyles are acceptable.
- Students adhere to guidelines around acceptable physical touch and personal space.
- Students are expected to complete and turn in homework daily.

- Students are expected to speak English during class time.
- Students use "looking eyes" and "listening ears" during class and raise their hands to share. Students do not talk among themselves or interrupt when others are speaking.
- Students do not raise their voices or shout during class time, lunch, or transition time inside the school building.
- Students make eye contact when addressed by the teacher.
- When students need support from the teacher, they raise their hand and ask for help.
- School and classroom rules focus on individual behaviors and rights rather than the larger community.
- Teachers track student attendance and punctuality daily.
- All stakeholders follow the proper procedure for reporting issues and concerns.
- Teachers communicate with caregivers via email or a virtual messaging platform and expect timely responses.
- Visitors to the school sign in at the front office and wear a visitor badge.

Select one rule or norm that resonates with you. It might be one that students appear to have a hard time adhering to, one in need of improvement, or one that you'd simply like to ensure is equitable and inclusive.

Reflect

Reflect on the following questions related to the rule or norm you've selected:

- Have you ever evaluated this rule or norm's effectiveness?
- Which social identities are likely to benefit most from maintaining this rule or norm?
- Which social identities are likely to struggle most with this rule or norm?
- Is the rule or norm's intended purpose actually fulfilled?

Resolve

Use the following resolutions to involve students in the process of reviewing the effectiveness of this rule or norm.

- Learn about the similarities or differences students recognize from parallel norms they follow in additional cultures they identify with. Allow them to consider cultures beyond ethnic cultures, such as sports, activities, family gatherings, and so on. This fosters a greater sense of respect and belonging for and among students. Moreover, you and your class will learn to view the concept of norms from more angles in a way that expands the potential for cultural proficiency. Finally, you just might hear an idea that could help rework the current rule or norm so that it is more inclusive, equitable, and productive.
- After presenting the benefits and drawbacks of the rule or norm, allow students to share their ideas for improvement.
- Share successes with colleagues so that they too might benefit from the process.
- Continue applying the 3*R*s method to other norms at any available opportunity. This could happen randomly, such as through moments of surprise, or by gradually working through the list of rules and norms presented above or in the iceberg model of culture in Figure 3.2 (p. 54).

With every practice of the 3*R*s, your critical consciousness's filtering abilities strengthen while simultaneously weakening the limitations posed by unconscious biases. This book will continue to provide you with opportunities to practice using the method, primarily focused on use within your school community. That said, practicing the 3*R*s in your ample daily experiences outside the educational setting will foster inestimable growth. Only then can you truly diversify and better comprehend incoming knowledge. Engaging in this practice regularly will increase your confidence that you are becoming a more culturally proficient educator and ensure that your positive influence extends beyond the classroom.

Review, Reflect, Resolve

A habit is first a wanderer, then a guest, and finally the boss.

—Hungarian proverb

Review

- Did any of your own experiences come to mind while reading this chapter? This could include a moment of surprise relating to students, caregivers, colleagues, or others; an exclusionary behavior you didn't recognize as such at the time but can now acknowledge; or an interaction in which you concluded that the reason behind someone's actions was the result of one identity (e.g., their sexual orientation, gender expression, ethnicity, or socioeconomic status).
- Choose one of these experiences now to apply the 3Rs to.

Reflect

After applying the 3Rs to gain more insight about the experience, what knowledge or gems of wisdom did you gain?

Resolve

- Follow through on the resolutions you created through your application of the 3Rs.
- Designate a method for keeping up this practice, as needed. Maybe you'll begin by putting a bright sticky note on your desk reminding you to pay attention to moments of surprise. Perhaps when an unconscious bias pops up, you create a quick reminder in your phone to alert you at a time when you can thoughtfully review, reflect, and resolve. You could walk through the steps on your way home, in the shower, while doing dishes, or any other time when you can engage in deep thought. Soon enough, you won't need the reminders because the exercise will become second nature and processing the 3Rs will require far less time. The wisdom gained from each

experience enhances your power to be your very own best teaching manual. Eventually, you won't need to rely on the method as often, and your consciously unbiased thoughts will naturally guide your actions.

One rain does not make a crop.

—Creole proverb

Huda's Responses

 HR12:

Have you encountered any exclusionary behaviors yourself? If so, are they regular or occasional occurrences? What is your reaction to exclusionary behaviors when they occur? If you rarely encounter exclusionary behaviors, how do you think you would react if you encountered them 10 times? 100 times? Which exclusionary behaviors stood out to you? Were they ones you've faced? Ones that you yourself have committed? Ones you've witnessed, not knowing they were harmful? Consider the response of the targeted individual(s) and reflect on why they may have had the reaction they had.

If you realized that you have committed an exclusionary behavior, join the club. Unconscious biases are the sneaky culprit. The good news is that the critical consciousness skills you will learn diminish the probability of its reoccurrence. You will get there, but it certainly won't happen overnight. I know that from experience.

In my days as a multilingual development specialist in schools, one of my tasks was to arrange access to translators for caregivers at school meetings. At this school, many of the families were Arabic speakers, as am I. During one such meeting, student work was displayed, and parents of all backgrounds walked around observing and discussing the projects. A couple of parents spoke to me in Arabic, and I made sure to introduce them to the translator and offer our services. The formal meeting was about to begin, so the translator and I began providing translation headphones to the caregivers in need. I noticed a woman dressed in hijab who lingered near a project and didn't follow the rest of the parents. Without hesitation, I walked over to her and, in Arabic, softly announced that the meeting was about to start and let her know that we had translation headphones available. She looked directly at me and said in English that sounded just like mine, "No thanks, I'm good. I was delayed at work and only arrived a moment ago. I just wanted to take a closer look at my son's work while everyone was still gathering." She gave a small, polite smile and went to take her seat. I felt like a fool.

To elaborate on how we are all prone to making these mistakes, here are some reasons why my exclusionary behavior surprised me. I am a Muslim and well versed in the stereotypes around that identity. Although I hadn't yet chosen to dress in hijab at that time, I had several close relatives and friends who did. I communicated with women in hijab all the time, with the vast majority never in need of translation services. This included a significant number of my students' mothers who dressed in hijab, reinforcing the norm in my work environment. Yet even with plenty of life experience to prove the stereotype wrong, my instinct reverted to the unconscious bias formed in my childhood—the one teaching me the notion that women wearing a head covering, especially Brown women, were "foreign" and probably unable to speak English. Unaddressed unconscious biases are pretty strong, folks.

I am not sharing this story to lessen your hope in your chances of overcoming biases. Instead, I want to illustrate how our real-world experiences, viewed with an enhanced lens, serve as the greatest lessons of all. The goal isn't to ensure you'll never make a mistake again. It is to identify and use every opportunity, including the mistakes you *will* make, to grow and become better. That was the outcome for me, and it didn't take me long to realize what the source of my blunder was.

Immediately after the meeting, I apologized to the parent and shared my reflections with her. She was very kind and told me that if she got a dollar every time she faced that particular exclusionary behavior, she could cut back to working part-time. She said that she sometimes took the opportunity to educate the initiator of the behavior and other times just didn't have the energy for it. Now that I dress in hijab, I can empathize. At a museum, on a plane, or in line at the market, I am never completely free of the pressure to interrupt the flow of my day to educate someone who commits an exclusionary behavior. "You speak English *soooo* well!" is one that is not only encountered by women in hijab. My friends who are Black, Brown, and of AAPI heritage are unfortunately well acquainted with this exclusionary behavior as well, perhaps especially in professional spaces. Another outrageous one that may be more particular to my experience is the wide-eyed *"You* drive?" If you are having a hard time believing any of these admissions, let me tell you, I only wish they were untrue. Now picture these occurring regularly, and we come to our next point.

Contemplating how you might respond to the 100th exclusionary behavior gives you the opportunity to imagine the effect not just on your stress level and mood but on how you would interpret communications. If you keep having to take shots fired at you, you learn to put your guard up. Keep this in mind when your student or the cashier at the store appears to be apathetic or on the defense when you were genuinely communicating thoughtfully and respectfully. In this scenario, it isn't your fault, but it isn't necessarily their fault, either. It is just one of the many ugly outcomes of rampant unaddressed unconscious biases.

[HR] **HR13:**

Select a cultural norm you've witnessed that differs from your own. If you can think of one from any of your students' cultures, choose one of those. How did you learn about this norm? How does the norm differ from your beliefs around the issue? Has your knowledge of this norm shaped any of your communications or practices?

We learn a lot through observation. When it comes to real-world nuanced learning about cultures, you must apply a filter to your observations. Using critical consciousness skills to filter through new information ensures you won't make the mistake countless educators make of reinforcing biases that disregard students' individuality and the complex diversity of all identities and cultures.

It is not just communities with recent demographic changes that have this problem. It happens just as much in schools where people from marginalized identities have belonged for decades. Even there, symptoms of undervaluing cultural proficiency are bound to appear. The storyline usually goes something like this: Without adequate learning resources provided, school staff members remain undereducated about the communities they serve. Therefore, unless they willingly do in-depth and unbiased research themselves, their conclusions are primarily derived from informal observations of students and families. Time marches on as the "minority" population increases and has now been a part of the community for several years or even decades. This is when the programmed hush tightens its hold, if it hasn't already. Staff, including school and district leaders, become reluctant to ask clarifying questions because they feel as though they should know the answers by now. Unresolved unconscious biases remain, yielding lower expectations, confirmation biases, exclusionary behaviors, disproportionate discipline, flawed communications with families, and more. Privileged identities—in terms of both race and influence, as in who holds leadership positions in schools, districts, and government—tend to produce denial of the realities occurring in classrooms. This continues to hold true as staff's remarks and actions prove they need learning opportunities that inform and guide them toward cultural proficiency. Adding insult to injury, disenfranchised communities are unequipped to effectively advocate for students. And all the while, teachers continue teaching the only way they know how: in a way that is culturally biased in favor of privileged identities. Of course, we now know that even privileged identities receive a lower standard of education from this sort of instruction. But when education perpetuates systemic oppression, excluded identities are most likely to be stamped with unqualified labels and considered at risk. And the cycle continues.

Throughout this timeline, there are undoubtedly educators who are culturally competent by their own means. They are the ones creating a positive legacy, whose students will remember them with love and respect. Unfortunately, these staff members' cries for reform are dismissed or even ridiculed. I have met far too many educators who have experienced this. They are ever frustrated not just by the lack of support but by having to witness otherwise preventable prejudice and inequities. In the end, the feeling of defeat is shared by all.

I realize that this paints a bleak picture. I wish it weren't true, but it is a common reality in schools—maybe even yours. But examining the picture releases its lessons. The following example comes from Laura, a school principal who uses such lessons to glimpse the light at the end of the tunnel.

Laura's school includes a significant number of students whose native origin is Mexico. Through observation and conversation with many students, she learns that they were each given a nickname by their families. Some students insist that giving nicknames is a common tradition among *all* Mexicans. Several parents confirm this.

One week, Laura is at an education conference and engages in a fantastic discussion with a social worker named Carlos. Upon learning that he is Mexican, she brightly asks what his nickname is. He tells her that he doesn't have a nickname. Confused, she explains that her students and their parents told her that *all* Mexicans are given nicknames. Carlos's smile fades as he tells her that Mexicans are a diverse group of people who live in different places and hold a variety of beliefs. Laura's face turns bright red. Carlos sympathetically explains that the nicknaming norm is common among many Mexicans he knows, and he's sure that her students and their parents' experiences led them to the conclusion they shared with her. Nonetheless, it is not true for every single Mexican, and to believe that one norm is the same for all people can put you on dangerous ground.

Laura feels humiliated and, as she puts it, "dumb as a rock!" She senses her kneejerk reaction of defensiveness kicking in. With courage and vulnerability, she tells Carlos exactly how she is feeling, concluding that these sorts of mistakes allow her to learn and grow. Carlos's smile reappears. With compassion, he tells her that her generalization is nothing compared with the hurtful stereotypes he's met with in both professional and social settings.

Laura was able to process the 3Rs around the experience before she shared it with me. She successfully applied her resolutions to teaching, learning, and communications, resulting in several proud moments that she excitedly shared. For example, she resolved to include "maybe" in any conclusions she drew about unfamiliar cultures so that she would avoid making similar inaccurate assumptions in the future. Her resolutions resulted in positive side effects: her active modeling of this strategy led to teachers and then students following suit. She beamed with joy when I reminded her that those lessons had the power to reverberate endlessly. We agreed that in the end, her awkward moment with Carlos had paved the way to rich rewards.

 HR14:

Can you speak more than one language? Do you speak the additional language your ancestors spoke? Why or why not? Did your caregivers encourage you to learn or speak another language? Do you wish you could speak an additional language?

I grew up speaking another language that I sadly did not value until adulthood. In fact, as a child I was ashamed that my parents spoke English with an accent. During my childhood, I witnessed the discrimination they faced on account of ignorant biases toward their accents. Thinking about it still tugs at my heartstrings. I hope that with your help, fewer children will be robbed of feeling justified pride about their culture and languages. Rather than looking down on those who speak with an accent, people should be impressed. An accent means the person speaks more than one language, and that is impressive!

Whether or not you are multilingual, sharpening your empathy skills will prove useful for you and the community you serve. Using your all-powerful imagination, picture a scenario in which, for some urgent reason, you and your loved ones must move to another country. You are unfamiliar with the culture and the language there. If you don't have children of your own, imagine that any younger loved ones are with you. In their new school, their entire education is in a language that is foreign to them. To their relief, they find there are a few other students in their class who are native English speakers. Their classmates have a range of understanding in the new language. You, too, want to learn the new language and decide to take a course in it. Fumbling through this unfamiliar language is a sobering experience that takes your confidence level down a peg. When you do meet others who speak your home language, you feel a great wave of relief. It feels amazing to be able to speak comfortably, fluently, and in a way that shows your intelligence and personality.

Fortunately, your teacher and your young ones' teachers prove to be great cheerleaders who know that retaining and promoting the use of your first language can help increase your proficiency in the new language. Your new country's society values multilingualism and sees it as a benefit to you and everyone else who lives there. Hence, your teacher highly encourages you and your English-speaking classmates to use English when needed to discuss concepts and support one another in learning vocabulary in the new language. Access to your metalinguistic skills around English enhances your comprehension of the new language. You are also pleased that you can easily find information about news and events and other communications in English. When important events and meetings occur in your young ones' school, you can attend without hesitation, knowing that you will be welcomed and supported there. Their school has made it clear that your inclusion is valued through equitable practices that encourage your participation. Both environments set up your family to thrive, and that is what you do!

Now, imagine that the opposite is true—that your home language is not valued in this country. You and your children are not permitted to use English to increase your understanding of new vocabulary and concepts. You feel unsupported and awkward not just in your own learning environment but also in that of the children in your life. Information is not always translated, making you feel disconnected and helpless. Judging from the glares and comments of strangers, expressing yourself in your home language outside the classroom appears to be equally unwelcome. Although you're pleased to find that your younger loved ones appear to be learning the new language, you're noticing a gradual change in their attitude toward their home language. They are avoiding using it and dismissing it as unimportant and even unfavorable. Because language is embedded in culture, this deteriorated value is apparent in the norms they exhibit and is no longer aligning with the values you honor and had hoped to pass on to the next generation. You are frustrated, lonely, and depressed. All in all, you don't feel able to confidently pursue employment, social events, or involvement in your young ones' school. The inequities you're facing have tainted all opportunities in the new land you call home. Yet apathetic dialogues from influential, privileged voices swiftly blame you for your limited contributions to society.

The former scenario is clearly preferable to the heart-wrenching latter. If you haven't realized it already, it's important to do so now: the latter scenario is the lived truth for far too many families today. Consider how this might be relatable to people in your school community. For those who you've seen succeed in such environments, consider the incredible strength and resilience they needed to achieve that success. Revisiting this sample scenario and inviting others to do the same will enhance your empathy skills—and your legacy, community of advocates, and larger community will be better for it.

6
Stepping Up
Actions to Confront Bias Across Your School

If you think you're leading and no one is following you, you are only taking a walk.

—Afghan proverb

You have reached the point in your journey where it's time to put all your learning—about unconscious bias, the cultural proficiency continuum, privilege, cultural responsiveness, exclusionary behaviors, and critical consciousness—into practice. In this chapter, we pull it all together and explore how to extend your cultural proficiency in your school community through reflection and dialogue.

Let's first discuss what shape that dialogue will take. Throughout this book, our conversations have allowed us to pass the ball back and forth as we get closer to our goal of cultural proficiency. Bouncing ideas around with others and reaching out to them for mutual support will certainly aid your continued learning. Remember, though, to remain thoughtful about how you ask and to whom you go for that support. It is not the job of marginalized people to educate you. Systemic oppression and exclusion in education systems did them great harm, and as your growing cultural proficiency and awareness of your privileges will help you understand, placing this additional task on their shoulders adds to their heavy burden. This is not to say that their presence and voices are not invaluable in your learning process, because they absolutely are. People generally want to share their stories. But it is important that when they do, it will be by their choice, with a feeling of confidence that they will not be met with reprimands or ignorant and frustrating feedback.

I advise against approaching learning opportunities, planned or not, with a blank sheet of paper expecting others to spell it all out for you, which would point to unacknowledged privilege and possibly insult already injured parties. (If you need a refresher, **HR10** [p. 85] illustrates how such a scenario played out through Joe's perspective.) When you do the work first, those potential troubles evaporate.

To be clear, the "work" I refer to can be thoroughly enjoyable. I believe countless educators share my joy in learning about and from various cultures and perspectives. If you seek them out, you will find a plethora of rich resources that teach from the viewpoint of commonly excluded voices. For example, you might seek out books to expand your knowledge around dismantling systems of injustice; individual memoirs and narratives that offer sliding doors into the world experienced by those with identities or experiences that differ from your own; or fiction that spotlights underrepresented identities. Other media, such as radio, TV, and film, also enable us to see and hear diverse perspectives directly from the people who hold those identities—a relatively recent development, since those stories used to be told almost solely by people of dominant identities. Public media—mostly radio and television stations—produce excellent free learning programs from a variety of viewpoints and experiences. Documentaries can provide us with hard facts supported with visual evidence and compelling commentary. Some to check out are *13th* (DuVernay, 2016), *Miss Representation* (Siebel Newsom, 2011), *Bowling for Columbine* (Moore, 2002), *Reel Bad Arabs: How Hollywood Vilifies a People* (Jhally & Earp, 2006), and *Who We Are: A Chronicle of Racism in America* (Kunstler & Kunstler, 2021). *The United Shades of America* is a documentary series on CNN following comedian W. Kamau Bell's explorations of communities throughout the United States and the challenges they face. Even sitcom writers are finding ways to creatively weave teachable moments into shows like *The Neighborhood* and *Black-ish*.

Social media platforms and websites also offer a plethora of options for exploration. For example, websites like www.learningfor justice.org are devoted to providing educators with resources for culturally responsive practices, lesson plans, professional development tools, and more. Offline, excellently curated museums immerse visitors in experiences certain to leave a powerful impression.

These examples barely scratch the surface of what's out there, and my intention here is not to provide a comprehensive list of resources. Ultimately, those who seek out this learning will find endless possibilities as each resource opens new doors. I currently have my own list of "must-see/read/try" items that I just can't get ahead of. It is the only "to do" list that I am thrilled to see getting longer.

The ideas and insights you gain from this learning will pull you in a new direction and allow you to set your eyes on sights formerly unseen. Your continually clearer lens will grant you magnificent, expanded views. This work creates a base of knowledge that can serve as a jumping-off point to thoughtful communications with people of all identities. When you have opportunities to learn directly from people with marginalized identities, the background knowledge you've attained sets the stage for more sophisticated learning that will diversify and enrich your education. These more thoughtful learning opportunities will be devoid of stereotypical beliefs and exclusionary behaviors, making for a more enjoyable and productive outcome for both parties. I am not alone in experiencing joy and renewed hope after meeting people who took responsibility for doing the preliminary work on their own, even if just to gain a basic level of understanding. The dialogues that ensue emanate respect, empathy, and humility. These are what culturally proficient conversations look like.

Expanding your ability to engage in productive learning empowers you to consciously take more meaningful action steps—including using your privileges to open minds and doors that allow others in. For example, one privilege might be having a seat at the table where decisions are made. You could use that privilege to remind others at the table of the importance of including and listening to often-excluded perspectives. Inviting those identities to the table is necessary to broaden possibilities and cultivate equity, inclusion, and greater achievement for all.

Advancing your awareness around biases and privileges is vital to attaining cultural proficiency. Throughout this book, you have done a lot of that work, which now places you in a prime position for these final chapters. Naturally, if you haven't already jumped into significant practice within your school community, you may still feel a bit hesitant. I get it. Some of us can come up with 1,000 reasons and excuses for why it's not the right time. Yet maintaining a sense of urgency is a necessity for maximizing not just your own potential but that of your entire community. The key is to remain focused on what you *can* do. Then you are guaranteed to see that list grow until there is little you *can't* do.

To help you get over the hurdle, I want to offer a gentle push. In this chapter, I have compiled 11 statements or scenarios that educators are likely to encounter in schools. As with the Connect and Converse prompts in the previous chapters, you will read and reflect on each, and I also provide my perspective. These are more outward focused than the previous prompts, however, to help you practice preventing and responding to common pitfalls that may otherwise interrupt your advancement. Each statement is purposely set on its own page; the blank space is aimed to encourage you to take a lengthened pause to deeply consider your response. The insight you gain will elevate your ability to take your consciously unbiased skills schoolwide to make your team larger, stronger, and more effective.

The following steps describe how you can use this chapter to get a pulse on your current readiness and as an ongoing resource to turn to for continued support in the future.

1. Review and respond to the statement or scenario provided. To really get an idea of your progress thus far, it is crucial that you reply fully before looking at my response.

2. Reflect on the emotions, beliefs, and actions that you would respond with if you faced the statement or scenario in the moment.

3. Check out my response to see how it compares with yours. You may find, even if your own response is acceptable, that my response further expands your funds of knowledge and enriches your plans. Resolve to fulfill any practices that are applicable to you and your school community. Make note of your commitments in the index you created, your schedule, or anywhere else that will help you ensure you get them done.

4. In your online or written calendar, schedule a reminder to circle back to this chapter every now and then. It will call on you to take a step outside your hectic day-to-day so that you can touch base with the true heart of your career as an educator. This is when you can check in on your progress with the resolutions you had set, celebrate accomplishments, and advance to strategies you were not able to enact the last time you were here (e.g., taking next steps in a particular area, bringing more colleagues into the fold, or taking a cue to dig into your research or notes from the index you created at the start of this journey). Keeping this regular check-in will boost your confidence and motivation to keep taking those world-changing leaps!

Your new students' previous teacher
"fills you in" about what to expect of a
particular student or group,
and it is not good.
(See **HR15** on p. 151.) [HR]

"I regularly assess my biases through the 3*R*s, but I wouldn't say I'm culturally proficient yet. I just don't feel ready to act before I feel fully prepared."
(See **HR16** on p. 154.) ⬚HR

**"I AM NOT GOING TO CARE MORE THAN
THEY DO. THEY NEED TO STOP WHINING
AND JUST WORK FOR IT LIKE
THE REST OF US DID."**
(See **HR17** on p. 158.) HR

"Classroom décor is overrated. My classroom is decorated in the way I've always done it. If it ain't broke, don't fix it." (See **HR18** on p. 161.) ⬚HR

"They are working below their potential, and their grades show it."
(See **HR19** on p. 162.) HR

"I feel like we are always being forced
into a new program. I understand the
importance of culturally proficient
practices; I just don't have the time
or energy to implement
a whole new curriculum."
(See **HR20** on p. 163.) (HR)

"Their parents don't show up to anything, which leaves
me doing more work because they don't want to."
(See **HR21** on p. 167.) HR

[silence]
(See **HR22** on p. 169.) HR

"This is the way we do things here.
If they don't like it, they can go
back to where they came from."
(See **HR23** on p. 171.) HR

"That's reverse racism. Imagine if we
had a White History Month or a
White Entertainment Channel.
We would never hear the end of it."
(See **HR24** on p. 174.) HR

"I am very confident about my abilities as a culturally proficient educator. How can I take my self-assessments to the next level?"
(See **HR25** on p. 175.) [HR]

Your Ever-Growing Capacity

I hope that the process of responding to the statements or scenarios in this chapter has given you the confidence you need to forge ahead. Maintaining urgency in your commitment to the resolutions you've set is essential to creating real change. Your legacy of action will break through the stagnant arguments sustaining the status quo that ultimately hurts us all.

Remember that this chapter isn't your only ongoing resource to turn to throughout your journey toward cultural proficiency. There are several big ideas commonly encountered in schools that are addressed in previous chapters, including shame's power to halt progress (Chapter 1), the tendency to dismiss or blame targets of discrimination and hate crimes (Chapter 2), discrimination against Emergent Multilingual Learners (Chapters 2 and 5), beliefs in false structures such as meritocracy and color-blindness (Chapter 3), the importance of acknowledging race and the effects of privilege (Chapter 4), and exclusionary behaviors (Chapter 5), among other themes. The research, examples, and prompts are all there to prepare you with the information you need to respond knowledgeably and thoughtfully.

Finally, don't forget that you also have additional ideas about these topics in the personal index you created. This might be a good time to step back and consider all you've accomplished since the start of your journey. Your capacity has surely grown, and it is deserving of the sense of accomplishment I hope you have. There will be more to come as you inspire others to take this wondrous and fulfilling journey as well. I am truly excited for you and hope that you feel the excitement, too!

Review, Reflect, Resolve

An ounce of prevention is worth a pound of cure.

—Korean proverb

Review

- What were your emotional reactions to the statements or scenarios and the responses provided?
- Do the outcomes help you feel confident moving toward actionable change?

Reflect

- What might your reactions indicate about where you currently stand on the cultural proficiency continuum?
- Which areas do you feel you might need more work on?
- Which strategies do you feel confident enough to begin executing immediately?

Resolve

- Dig deeper to identify any sources of difficult emotions that arose around certain topics so that you can become better equipped to address them and improve your capabilities overall. For example, you might conduct further research and learning, engage in discussions with culturally proficient colleagues, and work through why and how a given topic is a trigger for you based on experience. (See pp. 43–45 [life experiences, in **HR5**] and Chapter 4 [privilege].)
- Select which suggestions you will try out first and schedule them in your calendar or action plan.
- Follow step 4 from page 136 for returning to this chapter for regular check-ins with your resolutions to ensure that your progress is unimpeded. Remember that the awkwardness and intensity will absolutely lessen over time. Every round of 3*R*s you practice and every objective you attempt build your

repertoire and proficiency level, setting your course on far smoother waters ahead.

Knowledge is a shining light, skills a flowing spring.

—Uyghur proverb

HR15:

Your new students' previous teacher "fills you in" about what to expect of a particular student or group, and it is not good.

Action Step: **Cultivate consciously unbiased expectations.**

"Teachers can be mean." I was a classroom teacher when I first heard my brother make this statement. Because he was always commending the work of educators, it came as a surprise.

"You must be joking, right?" I asked. He agreed that he was, mostly, but his comment sadly held a kernel of truth. He explained that although he had had some great teachers, they certainly hadn't shown up in his life in masses. To provide some context, my brother's exceptional academic career and top scores on his medical board exam paved the way for his being the successful physician he is today. This might come as a surprise to many of his former teachers and principals. In school, he had a hard time remaining engaged, although he was able to correctly respond to teachers' questions even when he was off task. He was privileged with educational resources and a strong support system at home as well as remarkable intelligence, noticeable from his earliest years. These qualities did not lessen his teachers' frustrations, however. Rather than seeking out methods for meeting the needs of advanced learners, his teachers instead handed down disciplinary actions for his fidgeting and lack of focus.

He told me that the worst part of it was the poor reputation that grew out of these measures, which followed him from year to year, the stories about him passed from one teacher to the next. He explained that at the start of every new school year, he was filled with hope that he might hit the reset button to finally prove himself. And every year, his hopes were dashed when yet another new teacher made it clear that they "had their eye on him." With low expectations set from the start, he felt that no matter what he did, he would be the first to be blamed and punished. It wasn't exactly motivating, nor did it do anything to improve his off-task behaviors.

Fortunately, his ability to thrive academically placed him in advanced placement high school courses. Coming from a K–8 school, high school offered him the fresh start he'd prayed for. He met school staff whose expectations for him were based solely on the fact that he had done well enough to be placed in their classes. He shared some words from a few teachers and administrators who had clearly held higher expectations for him, which he in turn met. My heart was warmed by his appreciative tone of voice—and broke a little that he hadn't encountered these educators sooner.

My heartbreak continued upon hearing similar declarations from students I interviewed in my consulting career. Regardless of their academic standing or past behaviors, they were all desperately crying out for a fresh start. Many lacked the privileges that turned out to be my brother's saving grace. Especially for those living in underresourced homes, having a second chance in a culturally proficient school might be their only prospect for achieving their full potential. I suppose their teachers hadn't encountered a testimony like the one my brother shared with me.

Fortunately for me and my own students, after I heard my brother's story, I made sure to take any suggestions and opinions from my students' former teachers with a grain of salt. In other words, I applied the "maybe" rule to their words of wisdom: *Maybe* this information will be helpful at some point, but for now, all my students will start with a clean slate. Although I value other teachers' thoughts, we are individuals with varied beliefs, practices, and communication styles. I couldn't reasonably predict that my unique relationships with students would be the same as theirs. In fact, I refused to believe they would be the same.

One of the best things I did as a teacher was to maintain this belief and state it repeatedly to my students. Like us, students want to be treated with respect. We are all continuously growing, learning, and deserving of the opportunity to show our capabilities without bearing the weight of previous mistakes or misunderstandings. The academic and behavioral outcomes of this practice were exceptional, and even now I receive notes of thanks from previous students.

Applying similar attitudes toward school staff and caregivers can be just as powerful. It's true that we can't expect an easy journey or a drastic transformation from every student or colleague we were warned about. There will aways be issues, past and present, outside our control. So stay tuned into what you *can* control. I had some memorable instances that tested my patience, but they were a measly price to pay for the gratification of giving people a fresh chance to write their own story.

You can cultivate consciously unbiased expectations by taking the following actions:

- Ensure that your expectations are not unduly influenced by...
  - Identification labels.
  - Former assessment scores.
  - Input from others.
  - Confirmation biases.
  - Previous experiences, including (but not limited to) interactions with the student's family members or friends or individuals with shared identities or characteristics or similar appearances.
  - Knowledge of former behaviors. Whatever happened occurred in the past, likely with other circumstances at play. None of those factors absolutely determines who the student is today.

- Ensure your and your student's potential for success by...
  - Learning what the source of the current issues might be.

— Evaluating whether your practices are affecting their ability to demonstrate their full potential (are you providing differentiated instruction, accommodations, social-emotional supports, healthy culture and community, and so on?).

— Treating your student like they are your "favorite" and seeing what the outcomes are. I think you'll be pleasantly surprised!

Anguish is our worst adviser.

—Chilean proverb

 ## HR16:

"I regularly assess my biases through the 3*R*s, but I wouldn't say I'm culturally proficient yet. I just don't feel ready to act before I feel fully prepared."

Action Step: **Cultivate consciously unbiased relationships.**

All right, no one's asking you to pull out the picket signs and markers. Making big moves toward growth and success for all doesn't necessarily require actions that risk losing your voice or your job. There are countless ways to make gains that start with simply expanding on your current practices. The prime place to begin is building relationships with students, which is essential to attaining and teaching cultural proficiency. You cannot fully achieve either goal—strong relationships with students or cultural proficiency—without the other. Conveniently, the most valuable resource in this area is one you already have: students.

An excellent way to begin is to make a sincere effort to say students' names the way they want them to be said. This is an instant declaration of respect. If you knew anything about me before picking up this book, you were probably aware of my passion for using names to build communitywide cultural proficiency. Names are a common denominator among humans, and the lessons they hold tap into several concepts addressed

throughout this text. Claims that one just can't possibly pronounce an unfamiliar name are a symptom of privilege and the
programmed hush. Names are derived from different languages,
some with unfamiliar sounds. Sometimes educators seem content to commit the exclusionary invalidation of being unwilling
to correctly pronounce them. Unconscious biases reveal themselves through notions of supremacy that indicate which names
are worth practicing and saying accurately. Educators who hast-
ily choose to turn Alejandro into Alex because the former is "too
hard to say" are often, ironically, the ones gracefully rolling out
names like da Vinci, van Gogh, Freud, Hippocrates, and Michel-
angelo. I have also too often heard that believing in the equal
value of *all* names is giving in to the so-called hypersensitivity
of people whose parents should have just chosen an *"American
name."* This perception oozes with privilege and bias. Using
your critical consciousness, pause to consider which names
tend to fall under that description. It shouldn't take long to recognize the connection to White supremacy—or to see the irony
when most children in the United States are *not* White, and the
land's original owners are Brown.

Making the effort to pronounce difficult or unfamiliar names
involves courageous and vulnerable practice. *Not* making the
effort will lead traditionally excluded students to absorb the
notion that tamping down their identity is a necessary reality to
be accepted in society. This symptom of cultural incapacity has
echoes of ancestors who were pressured or forced to change
their names to assimilate into mainstream society—and sends
a clear message that these students' identities pose an incon-
venience to the privileged among us. Yet not bothering to fully
learn students' names can more accurately be seen as a missed
opportunity for all. Names hold histories, identities, traditions,
and truths that can enhance communitywide growth and success. I have personally met scores of educators for whom this is
the case—and not only educators with marginalized identities.
In the learning opportunities I facilitate that focus on names,

many teachers attest that their family name once sounded "too German" or "too Irish." Encouraging them to recall this history and connect it to their students' present can help them tap into their empathy.

Learning centered around names helps groups overcome the programmed hush through a topic that relates to everyone and holds infinite learning opportunities. Name stories should be shared with the focus on whichever topic resonates most with the individual—examples include accurate pronunciation, language origin, the purpose of the name choice, the name's meaning, name-giving traditions in the person's cultures, identities the name represents, and any other related information. You could first conduct this activity during staff collaboration time to strengthen relationships; you might be surprised by some of the responses you get. You can then plan communitywide implementation to ensure the maintenance of name-valuing practices. My children's book, *Teach Us Your Name* (Essa, 2016); my TEDx Talk, *Your Name Is the Key!* (Essa, 2018); and other related resources can be accessed from my website (https:// culturelinksllc.com) to make implementation easy.

Consciously unbiased relationship building requires diversification—the final step in the three-step process toward cultural proficiency that involves expanding your knowledge, abilities, and reach. Day-to-day filtered observations are wonderful, but explicit data collection is equally important. Questionnaires are a helpful and relatively easy way to take inventory and better understand your students' backgrounds and identify their interests, strengths, and any accommodations they may need. They also show students your desire to build thoughtful and caring relationships with them. You should fully explain the prompts, provide opportunities to ask questions, and ensure students understand how the information serves both you and them. The following are some topics to consider for your prompts:

- Accurate name pronunciation
- Significant people in their lives, including housemates and roommates, caregivers, parents, family, friends, and other loved ones
- Human resources, including helpers with schoolwork, support, guidance, and companionship
- Responsibilities, including chores, jobs, or caregiving (e.g., caring for siblings or other loved ones)
- Usual schedule, including on weekdays, weekends, start of day, end of day, after school
- Locations, including where they currently live, whether they live in more than one home, places they previously lived
- Transportation, including modes of transportation, who accompanies them, how long they travel to get to school
- Religious, spiritual, and cultural practices and special days or holidays celebrated
- Feelings about school
- Learning preferences or ideal learning conditions ("I learn best when...")
- Obstacles to learning or completing tasks in or out of school
- Prior and aspirational goal achievement (academic, social, or personal)
- Issues within relationships with staff or students that are relevant today
- Anything you wish I knew

The last prompt should be an open invitation throughout the school year. Be sure to offer several means of sharing information to allow for differentiation among various communication styles, cultures, and circumstances. Encourage students to use the one that allows them to best express themselves. For example, you might provide a question or suggestion box or invite students to email or request a face-to-face chat with you.

Some of the greatest insights I've received from students came from notes tossed onto my desk when I wasn't looking.

Finally, keep in mind that the relationship-building process is multifaceted and ongoing. All topics included in this chapter will support your ability to cultivate authentic and effective relationships with and among students. Many can be used to support and strengthen partnerships with colleagues and care-givers as well.

 ## HR17:

"I am not going to care more than they do. They need to stop whining and just work for it like the rest of us did."

Action Step: **Cultivate consciously unbiased practices for cooperative learning.**

There can be countless reasons why students do not participate or show motivation in the classroom. By remaining focused on what you *can* do, such as building relationships and sustaining consciously unbiased expectations, you will surely see improvement. It's also important to continue checking any privilege-led thoughts, such as the notion that your students would succeed if they just worked harder or even if they "had what it takes"—leading you dangerously close to the myth of meritocracy.

Other key strategies to increase motivation and engage-ment lie in passing the mic to your students. Because although it's true in a sense that you shouldn't care more or work harder than they do, it is your job to guide them toward independence and motivation. You can achieve this by helping your students increase their collaborative skills, character, sense of belonging, and cultural competence. No teaching approach does this bet-ter than cooperative learning, which has students work together in small groups to maximize their own and one another's learn-ing. This frees you to engage in more individual and small-group support that elevates your connections to a whole new level.

Check out the following questions to assess and expand upon your current practices.

- Which of your current practices demonstrate your deep value of students as key stakeholders and contributors to the class's success?
- Do you consistently model positive practices, value students' feedback and participation, and respond to their needs with helpful support?
- Do students regularly teach and learn from one another?
- Do you work *with* students to establish clear, equitable expectations regarding procedures and policies (including, for example, transitions, group and partner work, independent assignments, character development, how to request support for various needs, and stress management)?
- How do you foster a healthy balance of high expectations and equitable practices?
- Do you consistently use positive self-talk and whole-group affirmations to build a sense of community, belonging, and self-esteem?
- Do you incorporate equitable and inclusive practices and participation methods to ensure all voices are included and heard (e.g., random response, think-pair-share, writing, use of students' additional languages, writing or drawing before verbalizing responses, wait time, use of symbols or signs indicating readiness to share)?
- Do you routinely include space and time for students to review and reinforce to them that collaborating with their peers enriches their learning experience? ("What knowledge or support did you receive from someone today?")
- Do you, with humility, discuss ways in which your social identities influence your worldviews and invite students to do the same?

- Do you enthusiastically encourage students to use their additional languages, including various English dialects, to...
  - Enhance comprehension of new terms by creating personal translations from their home language to the new language?
  - Communicate their thoughts and ideas with those who share their home language?
  - Teach a term or concept to those who do not know their home language?

- Do you teach and model conflict resolution skills?
- In what ways do you teach, model, and encourage vulnerability and humility?
- Do you regularly encourage students to access a variety of methods to communicate with you (e.g., through an anonymous format such as a suggestion box, one-on-one chats, or emails)?
- Are there established norms, created *with* students, to encourage honest, open, productive communication and learning?
- Do all students understand that they have the opportunity to create a fresh start for themselves and others? (In addition to students often needing a fresh start, sometimes their lived experience or preconceived notions may require them to offer a similar opportunity for others, such as school staff or classmates, to release any residual weight that may be holding them back from truly moving forward.)
- Do you model effective goal setting and steps to attain them? Goal-setting categories to consider include personal growth, social skills, health and wellness, community building, and academic growth.

The rope breaks where it is thin.

—Kazakh proverb

HR18:

"Classroom décor is overrated. My classroom is decorated in the way I've always done it. If it ain't broke, don't fix it."

Action Step: **Cultivate a consciously unbiased learning environment.**

Classroom environment affects students' performance. I wish I had known that when I was a classroom teacher. I recall that when a colleague of mine would leave a room, she'd jokingly say she was off to go "find her desk." I could empathize. The piles of papers, books, and materials on my desk matched the disarray of scattered student work and posters I put up on my walls. I did make sure to include elements that made my classroom welcoming, cozy, and colorful, so I thought I was all set. I didn't realize, though, that these elements represented and favored individualistic cultures over collectivist cultures. One example was a bar chart indicating the entire class's reading levels. Each student was given a code to anonymously identify their standing in the lineup. I thought this was a harmless way to promote healthy competition and boost those scores. I now see that what I thought was positive encouragement may have been working against the mantra I enthusiastically repeated to students: "Teamwork makes the dream work!"

Through the much clearer reflections in my rearview mirror, I now see how a shift in my thinking could have made all the difference. The reality is that students' environments create positive or negative reactions in their brains. Neuroceptive mechanisms check that these environments are socially, physically, and intellectually safe. When that is established, students achieve a comfortable alertness and are geared for optimal learning. When students are instead immersed in environments that exclude their cultural values or project indirect exclusionary behaviors, their brains go on alert and produce stress, which triggers defensive strategies (Hammond, 2014). To be sure you are cultivating a consciously unbiased learning environment, reflect on the following questions:

- Do students see "windows and mirrors" distinctly and widely presented in their school and classroom environment, including...
  - Classroom and hallway décor representing multicultural, collectivist values and visual aids? Some examples are classwide goals; team-building affirmations and encouraging words and sayings in students' additional languages; accents or colors and artistic styles that represent students' additional cultures; family or national origin photos or other items students can bring from home that represent their identities; and images or work from diverse contributors and heroes, including young people who led social movements.
  - Accessible and equitable spaces? Some examples are ample and safe spaces mindful of mobility and physical limitations; all-gender private bathrooms; nursing rooms; and quiet reflection rooms for prayer, meditation, and sensory peace.

- Is your classroom arranged in a way that promotes consciously unbiased cooperative learning by fostering visibility, open discussion, and accessible collaboration?

When the palace burns down, a better one can rise up.

—Yoruba proverb

 HR19:

"They are working below their potential, and their grades show it."

Action Step: **Cultivate consciously unbiased assessment and grading.**

Let's again turn our attention to what you *can* do rather than to factors beyond your control. We've addressed the value of relationship building, cooperative learning, and consciously unbiased environments. Another important step when students' performance is lagging is to analyze how equitable and inclusive your assessment and grading practices are. Some recommendations for cultivating consciously unbiased assessment and grading include the following:

- Grade based solely on academic performance so that attendance, homework completion, and behavior do not unfairly affect students' grades.
- Allow students to retake assessments and make up incomplete work.
- Offer opportunities to exhibit advanced understanding of concepts.
- Ensure lessons yield the greatest potential for success by being engaging and interactive and supporting various learning preferences and modalities, assessing and building on background knowledge, relating topics to real-world experiences, and scaffolding instruction to meet the needs of all learners.
- Use other strategies from this chapter to increase students' learning readiness and mitigate factors that could inhibit accurate assessment measurements, such as test anxiety and overall social-emotional status.

He that wills not to feed a cat feeds the mice.

—Bulgarian proverb

HR20:

"I feel like we are always being forced into a new program. I understand the importance of culturally proficient practices; I just don't have the time or energy to implement a whole new curriculum."

Action Step: **Cultivate a consciously unbiased curriculum.**

Scores of educators are unacquainted with the fact that all teaching is already culturally responsive. Therefore, cultivating a consciously unbiased curriculum isn't piling more on but simply reassessing and then improving the effectiveness of your current practices. (If you need a quick refresher about this, see pp. 51–52.)

The largest strides you'll take toward increasingly evolved curricular practices require a willingness to reassess "the classics" that you grew up with. Unless you've been living under a rock for the last decade, you've likely heard of formerly celebrated books, authors, monuments, historical figures, and holidays that are now being reconsidered. Today's widespread and easily accessed breadth of information has opened the floodgates of truth, and the outcomes aren't always pretty. For many, these truths disrupt fond memories and perceptions, creating major discomfort. Understandably, it can be unpleasant to learn the unfortunate truth about a beloved book or the person one was taught to view as a hero. When it is something or someone we have enthusiastically endorsed in our classrooms, we feel an added ego-bruising twinge.

Some people get over this fairly quickly and make revisions moving forward. There are immense numbers of relevant unsung heroes who deserve to be highlighted in school curricula. To my delight, I have been finding that as awareness increases among media and content creators, more and more invaluable resources are becoming available. One such program created for schools by Teacher Created Materials is aptly named *Untold Stories*. It highlights the contributions of commonly excluded voices and identities, including those of journalists, philanthropists, entrepreneurs, inventors, and advocates of diverse backgrounds. Similarly, the program's thoughtfully curated collections of Culturally Authentic and Responsive Texts sets also feature "mirrors, windows, and sliding doors" that benefit all students while meeting content-area objectives.

If despite reading this far in the book you (or a colleague) still aren't persuaded to give up problematic nostalgia, then the reality might sting a bit. It boils down to privilege and insufficient empathy. Adamantly resisting cultivating a more consciously unbiased curriculum may indicate ignorance—an inability to recognize that biased learning harms *everyone*, not just those with excluded identities. Then there are those whose ignorance around the issue isn't the problem; quite the opposite. These individuals are highly aware of how well their unearned privileges have served them. In this case, fear is the culprit— fear that equity means they will have to give up their privileges. Rarely have I found people to admit this outright, but if you dig deep enough, it is sure to come to the surface. In these cases, unlearning and then cultural proficiency learning are called for. This can be attained through high-quality professional development and by engaging in books like this one.

Now, contrary to what many may be used to, positively repositioning your teaching and learning doesn't necessarily require an overhaul of materials. Remember that gaining cultural proficiency turns *you* into the supreme manual. Revolutionary revisions to your curriculum can be quite simple. Perhaps even without your realizing it, the knowledge you've gained throughout this book has polished the lens you use to analyze your practices, including the lessons, texts, and curriculum you use to teach your students. Keep in mind the following guiding questions when reviewing your curriculum and lesson planning:

- Does the lesson give your students access to "mirrors, windows, and sliding doors"?
- Search for bias in images or language. Are certain identities heavily represented in comparison with others?
  - Is information about often-excluded groups represented in tokenized ways, such as reducing women's contributions to science to a brief sidebar in a chapter that otherwise discusses only men's contributions to science?

- Are notions of what is important to learn about configured around the "West and the rest" (e.g., Western European nations heavily represented with the remaining majority of the world appearing as outlying countries with less significance)?
- In fiction literature and other media, who are the main characters versus the supporting characters and extras in texts and images? Heroes versus villains?
- Do images and language contain stereotypical features or actions?

• Search for bias in images or language. Is one group signified more positively than others?
- Who "conquers" and who "liberates" people of a land?
- Does the language used include degrading or offensive terms such as "the needy" or "uncivilized" to describe marginalized groups?
- When describing general actions, are pronouns used mostly masculine?

• Are you scaffolding and differentiating instruction to meet the needs of your diverse learners?

• Do students have opportunities to demonstrate and eventually model the skills they learn, such as practicing empathy and courageous vulnerability, learning from mistakes, and using critical consciousness?

• When applicable, are students guided to activate their rights through advocacy around the topic or others related to it (e.g., by writing letters to lawmakers, educating others, creating petitions and social media campaigns, attending live and virtual events to increase knowledge and support)?

You can answer many of these questions simply by observing your own lessons and curriculum with a keen eye. When you spot bias in a given text or see that certain inclusive strategies are missing, make the changes accordingly. Eventually, doing this will become second nature, making you a master of seamlessly reforming and upgrading any curriculum or program given to you.

> *Until lions have their own historians, accounts*
> *of the hunt will always celebrate the hunter.*
>
> —Nigerian proverb

 ## HR21:

"Their parents don't show up to anything, which leaves me doing more work because they don't want to."

Action Step: **Cultivate consciously unbiased caregiver communications.**

This sentiment is best responded to by establishing necessary systems of support for both students and caregivers in order to steer thinking away from resentment and toward an empathetic desire to understand. Remaining out of touch with the realities faced by disenfranchised communities will only make matters worse. In your own school or classroom context, focus your attention on the factors that may be limiting caregivers' abilities to become more involved. A good place to start is to evaluate the effectiveness of current communications and relationship-building efforts by contemplating the following questions:

- Are your communication methods accessible, equitable, and inclusive of a variety of caregivers' circumstances? Consider such factors as literacy, language and translations, schedules, transportation, physical abilities, and childcare.

- Have you gathered evidence (e.g., through diverse informal and formal feedback processes, data review for
  participation, and supplying resources necessary to
  increase participation and involvement) to ensure that
  families and caregivers of all cultural and linguistic
  backgrounds and identities feel welcomed as partners
  for student success?

- Are caregivers with marginalized identities motivated
  to participate in gatherings with others who share their
  distinct identity? Such events foster a greater sense of
  belonging while simultaneously strengthening school-
  to-home partnerships, building community, and creating
  systems of support. Some examples of identities to create events for include those who share the same home
  language, racial or ethnic identity, or underresourced
  status, as well as caregivers of students with disabilities.
  These events can be organized and run by caregivers or
  staff who share those identities with support from other
  school staff. For example, a Korean-speaking parent
  might make calls to invite the school's Korean families
  to a meet-and-greet where families create connections,
  share triumphs and challenges, and offer support to one
  another. Similar to what you would want your own experience to be (see **HR14**, page 128), they will be assured
  that using their home language at this meeting is welcomed and encouraged.

Another way to flip the switch on more traditional school
meetings is to pass the control to caregivers by assigning an
interpreter to translate thoughts and questions *into English* for
school staff instead of the other way around. This way, it isn't
caregivers huddled in a corner receiving translated announce-
ments from the school, but an open discussion where translators share insights directly from the families with the school
staff. In this freer and more equitable space, staff can answer

questions, learn about families' needs and rights, gain input to increase family engagement, and hear other helpful information. To keep up the momentum and increase further participation, a phone group chat could be created at the meeting. This would allow families to continue communications, request help, provide support, and plan future events. Others who weren't able to attend could be invited to join the group to expand its reach and encourage greater future participation.

> *In a battle between elephants, the ants get squashed.*
>
> —Thai proverb

HR22:

[silence]

***Action Step:* Cultivate consciously unbiased dialogue.**

In this book I have attempted to thoroughly illustrate how and why silence frequently manifests around the most important issues in education. This may be especially true in professional settings among staff. The power of the programmed hush is enough to bring even the most intelligent, dedicated educators to a halt. But remaining silent about challenging issues helps no one. It squashes prospects for equity and inclusion, makes everyone's job harder, and maintains the unjust status quo.

I have found that boldly addressing topics like race and discrimination is best done in structured dialogues that don't start out feeling so bold. To begin opening doors to these discussions, it is best to first inform staff why cultural proficiency is key to their success and to the achievement of their entire community.

I suggest recording staff members' input regarding the value of doing this work where everyone can see them. Eventually zeroing in on the prime objective of learning and growing together creates anchors you can refer back to in both difficult and triumphant moments. Moving forward effectively afterward requires establishing norms for constructive dialogue, a process that has been used successfully with not only staff but students as well. It fits in perfectly with cultivating a thriving cooperative learning environment. Creating and agreeing to a set of guidelines encourages productive participation, problem solving, and cultural proficiency. Once staff members have satisfactorily established the norms, they can record them on chart paper and post them in a highly visible location. I find it makes a meaningful impact when participants sign the norms.

Norms should be referenced whenever needed. I found them particularly helpful in initiating relevant topics, defusing the programmed hush, and effectively navigating emotionally complex conversations. Eventually, the guidelines will become common practice that participants can utilize confidently in and out of school, which only increases their chances of success.

I find that most guidelines arise naturally from the group creating them; the following were partially inspired by the work of Saunders and Kardia (1997) and Sensoy and DiAngelo (2014). The exact terminology used can be your (or the group's) own, but each of the following is important and worthy of being addressed and included:

- Practice and honor courageous vulnerability.
- Remain highly attuned to prohibiting shame's production of defensiveness and other adverse reactions.
- Understand that recognizing and learning from inevitable mistakes is key to the learning process.
- Expect temporary discomfort knowing the process is worthy and discomfort will be overcome through practice.
- Share the responsibility for including all voices. Those with a lot to say should be mindful of leaving space for others to contribute, and those reluctant to share should challenge themselves to allow others to hear their voice.
- Listen respectfully, being sure to never devalue people's experiences or lack thereof.

- Whenever possible, practice empathy skills to enhance your communication and comprehension.
- When you disagree, speak your truth. Be sure to challenge the idea, not the person.
- Maintain an open willingness to learn from others whose identities and experiences differ from yours.
- Check your assumptions. Recognize the circumstances that shape your beliefs, reactions, and any associated privileges that may limit your understanding of obstacles faced by others.
- Steadfastly distinguish opinions from informed knowledge. Everyone has opinions, but informed knowledge comes from research, repeated experience, and actions.
- Apply the "maybe" rule to learning focused on select identities. Also use this rule to release stagnant beliefs based on personal anecdotes.
- Show compassion, empathy, and support for one another toward your shared goal for learning and growing.

 HR23:

"This is the way we do things here. If they don't like it, they can go back to where they came from."

Action Step: **Cultivate consciously unbiased empathy skills.**

Unless the speaker of this statement is wholly Indigenous to the land they reside in, they are descended from people whose origins are elsewhere. Unless they were kidnapped and brought there, as was the case for enslaved people, their ancestors left their country of their own volition. These ancestors, like most immigrants today, were likely refugees or simply seeking greater opportunities and freedoms than they were afforded in their former land. As mentioned previously, those who identify as White can often trace their history back to people who experienced oppressions similar to those faced by immigrants in the United States today. A few examples of those nationalities include Irish,

Italian, Russian, and Turkish people, among many others; religions represented include Jews, Catholics, Muslims, and more.

By this point in your learning journey, I imagine you can see how the speaker's disconnect to their ancestral history stems from the same sort of culturally destructive ideas that they are now imposing on others. As you may recall was the case for me personally, the effects could very well extend to the speaker of the statement being Black or Brown or of AAPI heritage themselves. Still, the mighty unconscious biases they've attained have depleted their ability to empathize and see the matter clearly. This statement illustrates the false belief that the country they live in is *owned* by one dominant group and that therefore, the norms in place designed to benefit that one group should remain unquestioned, even if they obstruct "liberty and justice for all." Further evidence of apathy and ignorance appears in the blatantly biased behavior of telling people to go back to where they came from. It suggests that they believe everyone *can* go back without awful consequences, including loss of their livelihood or even their lives. The worst cases of apathy and racism are illustrated by those who *do* know the grave outcomes yet persist in their beliefs.

Whether stated ignorantly or defiantly, the beliefs communicated by this statement are filled with unacknowledged privilege that upholds notions of supremacy and threatens prospects for equity and inclusion. Using the guidelines for consciously unbiased dialogue (pp. 170–171) will help in relaying accurate information without resorting to blame. Building connections and knowledge is the most effective way to help you achieve your desired outcomes. Whether you are speaking to colleagues, caregivers, or students, responding productively prompts you to show empathy yourself. This will be very challenging in some cases, which is why it is important to keep in mind that the root of the issue is seldom individuals but structures. Creating systemic change is difficult to do alone. Effectual dialogues are helpful and can certainly yield progress, but they are no match for professional learning among an entire group. When an idea opposing cultural proficiency is revealed, it often means that others in that community hold the same opinion; they just might not be as vocal about it. Therefore, any instance deserves recognition for the red flag that it is. Although responding to an individual in the moment is important, take it as a cue for necessary widespread learning.

Starting with administrators, teachers, and other leaders in your school community, learning for cultural proficiency must be a priority. Professional development will bring more of these issues to light, amplifying potential for overall improvement. When held as a consistent priority, the expanded cultural proficiency and achievement of students, staff, and the entire community will be the reward that keeps on giving.

If you feel sure that your requests for cultural proficiency learning will not be met, I urge you to look for any opportunity to get closer to that goal. You could support your case by providing evidence (observations, research and data from this text and other sources, and data from your community) for why it would be beneficial. Testimonies from caregivers, staff, and especially students might be one of your most effective strategies for bringing the issue to the forefront of professional development planning. There are so many things you can do to promote awareness and action—something as small as forming your own book study with a few like-minded colleagues and eventually presenting the value of cultural proficiency learning to school or district leaders could help move the needle in providing PD to more of your school community—but I'll leave you with one more suggestion: encourage others with similar mindsets to make their voices heard, too. You never know: the individual who made the statement we are now responding to could end up being one of your greatest supporters once enlightened by your wisdom.

HR24:

"That's reverse racism. Imagine if we had a White History Month or a White Entertainment Channel. We would never hear the end of it."

Action Step: **Cultivate consciously unbiased awareness.**

"Reverse racism" describes racism experienced by dominant and historically privileged groups. Calling it "reverse" is adequate because the norm of racism is almost always pointed in the direction of Black, AAPI, and Brown people. The term is still problematic in more ways than one. I will first call it what it really is: racial discrimination. Due to present-day segregation, racial discrimination very well could impact the rare White student in a predominantly Black or Brown student population or neighborhood. The problem is that people who claim "reverse racism" imply that the effects are equivalent to those experienced by other groups. Although the White child in this sample scenario sadly encounters the negative effects of discrimination —it may foster bullying and will hurt their feelings—that is usually the full extent of it. The rest of the world mostly appears to hold their race supreme, and this will be supported by what they encounter nearly everywhere else, from their broad representation in the media and positions of power to their interactions in almost every other setting and system, including higher education, the workplace, legal systems, medical institutions, public spaces, and more. The racial discrimination they experienced is isolated and can't be compared to the racism others experience, which is widespread, institutionalized, systemic, and backed by policies and power that govern most of our lives and outcomes. To claim that racial discrimination is equal to racism felt by all others is ignorant and offensive.

The undermining inherent in this statement is also apparent in negative attitudes toward initiatives for equitable practices aimed at increasing diversity in higher education, the workplace, and the media. As you continue to hone your critical consciousness skills, your awareness of unacknowledged privilege will sharpen, as will your resolve to respond as effectively as possible. In the sample statement you read, the speaker is oblivious that there *are* White entertainment channels and White history months. They just aren't labeled that way because that describes nearly *all* of them, making them the norm. Cultural competence allows you to understand that providing normally excluded identities with representation is merely one equitable practice. It doesn't offer full equality but at least gives a small boost to marginalized groups, who continue to be left too far behind without the transport needed to catch up. Moreover, these practices are mostly exceptions found in small pockets, which only further proves that diverse identities are not equally distributed in the media or other centers of power.

You have likely already come up with some great responses in your initial reflection on this statement. Using the guidelines of consciously unbiased dialogue to express your thoughts as well as any of the additional information you read here will further boost your confidence and ability to enlighten the speaker. Because the statement requires addressing the concept of privilege, remember that Chapter 4 supplies you with many supportive examples and strategies for thoughtfully and effectively approaching the topic.

 HR25:

"I am very confident about my abilities as a culturally proficient educator. How can I take my self-assessments to the next level?"

Action Step: **Cultivate consciously unbiased behaviors.**

For this statement, I am going to respond as though you are the speaker. Let's assume you're in this position—that the examples of cultural proficiency in Chapter 2 describe where you are now. Your responses to the sample statements in this chapter have further boosted your confidence. You are now at the stage of regularly diversifying your learning and humbly welcoming other points of view. The following are suggestions for how you can gain even further insight through methods of observation and information gathering.

- Reach out to colleagues whom you consider culturally proficient and/or who have marginalized identities. Explain your goal and let them know that you want them to inform you of errors they witness you making that don't align with your goals.
- Video record yourself teaching a lesson. In the beginning, it is OK to watch the footage on your own. As soon as you can, invite a culturally proficient colleague to view it with you. There is a great deal of power in a fresh pair of eyes. This is not just to catch any negative points you may have missed but, just as important, to point out what you are doing right. We are often our own worst critics, and becoming hyperfocused on the negative is sure to tilt the direction of your path downward. Your journey should be exciting and rewarding!
- Before observing the recorded lesson, make sure you have the cultural proficiency continuum (p. 47) nearby for reference. Pause the recording as needed to jot down events and actions you might assign to the corresponding level on the continuum.
  - Are expectations and guidelines for student participation clear, equitable, and inclusive?
  - Is the verbal language and tone of voice used inclusive, asset based, and motivating for all students?
  - Are students' various learning preferences honored in the lesson and activity?
  - Is adequate wait time provided to increase students' potential for deeper comprehension, processing, and confidence in responding to or asking questions?
  - Are there improvements that could be made to enhance transitions?

— Regarding engagement and participation, which students are and are not actively engaged? Which actions or subjects increased or reduced engagement levels? How are students invited to participate? What improvements or accommodations might heighten participation and engagement for all students?

— Anything else worth noting?

Knowledge without wisdom is like water in the sand.

—Guinean proverb

7
Looking Ahead
The Journey Continues

Constant dripping hollows out the stone.

—Vietnamese proverb

This is it. The previous smudged lens through which you were taught to see the world has been polished to give you sharp clarity and unimpeded vision, and your evolution will continue to get easier over time. Nonetheless, you must never forget that this is a lifelong journey, and you should expect to trip over a crack or two on even the smoothest roads.

This was my experience, and one shared by culturally proficient folks all over. The critical consciousness skills I painstakingly cultivated kindled my passion and increased my store of wisdom, driving me toward this endlessly rewarding career. I was honored to be able to inspire and teach others to go on the journey as well. In my work, I taught about noticing and using moments of surprise and practicing the 3*R*s from my own successful experience, but I found I rarely had to use them anymore. I was quite confident in the superb filter I had created that would block out unconscious biases and prevent me from acting on any myself. One day, that confidence was given a shaking.

I was invited to facilitate a learning opportunity in a school district I hadn't yet worked with. We decided to focus on uncovering unconscious biases and identifying notions of supremacy. Driving in, I saw billboards and yard signs with covert and overt messaging that didn't positively align with my objectives. I didn't let it deter me. I tucked it away in my mind's "maybe" category and committed to giving the audience the same fresh start I would want. After all, I wouldn't want the signs on some of my own neighbors' lawns to represent me, so I refused to impose those assumptions on others.

Upon walking into the event space, my positive prediction was proven correct as I was welcomed by a group of warm educators. The initial activities were received with enthusiasm and engagement. Around the room, participants were leaning in, making eye contact, and nodding heads. Supportive comments and questions flowed, interspersed with reflective pauses around enlightening information. These were the usual uplifting outcomes I have the pleasure of witnessing when working with educators.

As excellent as this was, I couldn't help but notice an apparent outlier. Allow me to paint you a picture of this participant. He was a man of large, intimidating stature wearing a black leather vest and boots. His long, gray braided hair matched his goatee. Dark tattoos covered his arms and neck. He looked like the stereotypical image of a "biker dude." His demeanor aligned with that stereotype. The nods, smiles, and enthusiasm of his colleagues contrasted with his body language: head tilted back, unblinking eye contact, fierce facial expression. He leaned back in his chair, arms crossed, barely moving. He did not look happy to be there.

It was time for a break. Participants dispersed and mingled as I watched, smiling. Then I saw him: breaking through the crowd, the "biker dude" making his way toward my table. With a wave of fear, I felt my body tense up. I braced myself for what I felt sure would be a verbal attack on my presentation and my character.

Never breaking eye contact, he stopped abruptly at the table. His lips pursed and the stern look remained as he stood there shaking his head furiously. Startling me, he slammed both his hands down on the table. Then, to my surprise, his face broke into a smile. "Thank you so much! I was so *engaged* the entire time! I wish you could teach this to the entire world. You should just see what my family reunions look like. You'd see people of all backgrounds joined together in respect, love, and joy." He continued to express what was clearly a sincere appreciation of the messages I was sharing and went on to talk about his own experience and impressive actions as an advocate for social justice.

I was stunned—pleasantly so. I earnestly thanked him for his heartwarming words and encouraged him to share his story with the group after the break. He happily accepted and was just as passionate when sharing with the group. Afterward, when he returned to the same physical demeanor as before, I interpreted it accurately for what it was: focused attention and genuine engagement around learning that deserved to be taken seriously.

That evening, on my drive home, I activated my critical consciousness by applying the 3*R*s.

Review, Reflect, Resolve

It is no longer good enough to cry peace,
we must act peace, live peace, and live in peace.

—Shenandoah Native Indian proverb

Review

- This participant's appearance revealed a biased assumption I apparently held.
- His body language served as a confirmation bias of my mistaken assumptions.
- The combination of his appearance, his body language, and the context in which the experience occurred led to my conclusion that he was upset with my presence and presentation.
- My bodily reaction when he approached me reflected real fear.
- My tension, fear, and concern disappeared upon his verbal communications with me.

Reflect

- What biases led to my assumptions?

- What role did his appearance play in my assumptions? His hairstyle, facial hair, tattoos, and clothing contributed to my conclusion that he must be a biker. His body language further confirmed my stereotypical beliefs that he was probably an aggressive personality who disapproves of talk and actions around overcoming White supremacy, racism, and bigotry.

- How did my unconscious biases influence those conclusions? What exposure have I personally had to bikers?
  - My exposure to this identity has been limited mostly to media representation and occasional encounters on the road or other settings that do not allow for much communication. With little other than mass media portrayals to work from, negative unconscious biases were fostered. Bikers are primarily depicted as violent, racist alcoholics. Rarely was I exposed to multidimensional views that revealed their other identities. I couldn't recall learning about a biker's relationship with their parents, children, or neighbors. On the rare occasion that women were represented, similar characteristics were portrayed and further negatively typified by their acceptance of sexism, abuse, and other forms of oppression. Positive representation was rare, promoting beliefs that goodness in such individuals would be an exception to the norm.
  - As a result of the misrepresentation and subsequent unconscious biases, I felt discomfort and fear. Had this individual not approached me to engage in conversation, I doubt I would have had this epiphany.
  - I was taught to view this identity as drastically different from my own, making empathy and understanding more difficult to achieve.

Resolve
- Seek connections to help utilize empathy skills that will enhance my learning and future behaviors.

- Misunderstandings, fear, and hate due to exclusion and mis-representation are easily relatable to my experiences as an Arab Muslim woman who chooses to dress in hijab.
- Compare the instance to other issues that further expand the connections to be made. There are several other identities that could relate. It also applies to cultural norms such as clothing, body language, and gestures.

- Actively apply my critical consciousness to filter my observations of the identity. This will prevent confirmation biases from reoccurring and will allow me to give more people the benefit of the doubt.
  - Share the wisdom gained over time to enhance others' understandings and abilities as well.

The Journey of a Lifetime

The outcomes of the 3*R*s again proved worthwhile. Since I went through that process, I have purposefully engaged in communications with bikers or motorcyclists. Small gestures like a friendly wave and a "hello" receive a reciprocal response. My openness allowed for a few conversations here and there, as well. One transpired at a park where my mother, uncle, and I had arrived early to set up for a family gathering. We were disappointed to find that our reserved site's tables, which were originally placed close together, had been moved. The heavy picnic tables were now spread out and far from the central meeting spot. My mother and I were both nursing injuries, leaving us unable to safely help. The park was empty aside from a small group of motorcyclists, who appeared to be staring at us. I smiled and made a light remark about finding the tables moved. They immediately jumped up and walked toward me. This time, not an ounce of fear arose. They and my uncle began grabbing hold of the tables to carry them over our way. More family members arrived, shared in the task, and showed gratitude for the strangers' help. My learned openness and willingness to engage got us the help we needed and fostered a positive human connection for all parties. Best of all, it created an opportunity for a large group of people to witness acts of kindness unlikely discoverable through other means. I smile when I think of the beneficial moments of surprise that likely occurred as the now-busy park's visitors saw Brown Muslims casually chatting with White "biker dudes."

Of course, this doesn't mean that every experience I have with this identity or any others, including my own, is guaranteed to be positive. It merely sheds truthful light on the fact that when given the chance, people will prove that there is more good than bad and more core commonalities than differences among our fellow humans.

If I've had the pleasure of working with you in the past, you may have heard this story. Sharing the teachable moments from the experience allows me to continually adhere to the resolutions I committed to. Valuing both what we have in common *and* our differences will inspire abundant ideas and growth. In my case, my evolved appreciation for both human diversity and oneness planted seeds resulting in not just the facilitation of successful learning opportunities but also resources I've created, including my children's books, *Teach Us Your Name* and *Common Threads: Adam's Day at the Market*. Now, you may not be interested in a total career shift or in creating tangible resources, but trust that what you will go on to create will be resounding and honorable. Whether it leads to unforgettable relationships, lessons that resonate, or a legacy to be proud of, your cultural proficiency will surely foster undeniable progress.

The experience shared in this story and the related outcomes are a reminder that this exquisite journey is lifelong. Even when your acquired expertise has you gliding along the path you've paved, you should expect to encounter a few bumps. The beauty of this journey is that cultural proficiency creates ramps out of those bumps, consistently sending you soaring to greater heights.

I will be forever thankful that you took this journey with me. With genuine confidence, I softly release your hand as our conversation comes to a close. I am genuinely excited for you to continue this journey of a lifetime, inviting others to join you. My heart swells with joy at the thought of the bountiful learning and rewards that lie ahead for you. Most of all, I am filled with hope for the future of students, educators, and education as a result of your forward motion. As we each continue our shared march toward a better world, I hope we meet again, next time on a path crowded with fellow seekers of enlightenment and love.

Experience is the best teacher.

—Urdu proverb

References

Acholonu, R., & Oyeku, S. (2020, November 23). Addressing microaggressions in the health care workforce—A path toward achieving equity and inclusion. *JAMA Network Open, 3*(11).

Ahmed, R. (2021, June 10). *Muslim misrepresentation in film* [Video]. www.youtube.com/watch?v=Ssuhvv0l3bk

Akst, J. (2013, February 5). Some girls better at science. *The Scientist.* www.the-scientist.com/the-nutshell/some-girls-better-at-science-39813

Alvidrez, J., & Weinstein, R. S. (1999). Early teacher perceptions and later student academic achievement. *Journal of Educational Psychology, 91*(4), 731–746.

American Psychological Association. (n.d.). Confirmation bias. In *APA dictionary of psychology.* Retrieved December 1, 2023, from https://dictionary.apa.org/confirmation-bias

Artiles, A. J., & Ortiz, A. A. (Eds.). (2002). *English language learners with special education needs: Identification, assessment, and instruction.* Center for Applied Linguistics. https://files.eric.ed.gov/fulltext/ED482995.pdf

Bernhardt, S. (2014). *Women in IT in the new social era: A critical evidence-based review of gender inequality and the potential for change.* IGI Global.

Bishop, R. S. (1990, Summer). Mirrors, windows, and sliding glass doors. *Perspectives: Choosing and Using Books for the Classroom, 6*(3).

Boiko-Weyrach, A. (2017, March 21). Asian American students push to reveal what the "model minority" myth hides. *The World.* https://theworld.org/stories/2017-03-21/asian-american-students-push-reveal-what-model-minority-myth-hides

The Bridge Initiative. (2015). *The super survey: Two decades of Americans' views on Islam and Muslims.* Prince Alwaleed Bin Talal Center for Muslim-Christian Understanding, Georgetown University. https://bridge.georgetown.edu/research/the-super-survey-two-decades-of-americans-views-on-islam-muslims

Brower, T. (2021, September 19). Empathy is the most important leadership skill according to research. *Forbes.* www.forbes.com/sites/tracybrower/2021/09/19

/empathy-is-the-most-important-leadership-skill-according-to-research/?sh=
1cd7ad513dc5

Brown, B. (2015). *Daring greatly: How the courage to be vulnerable transforms the way we live, love, parent, and lead.* Avery.

Brown, B. (2017). *Braving the wilderness: The quest for true belonging and the courage to stand alone.* Random House.

Brown, B. (2022). *The gifts of imperfection: 10th anniversary edition.* Hazelden.

Castillo, J., Corbin, C., & Downer, J. (2019, March). *Implicit bias, exclusionary discipline, and expectations for students: Does the teacher-student racial/ethnic match matter?* Poster presented at the Biennial Meeting of the Society for Research in Child Development, Baltimore, MD.

Chemaly, S. (2015, February 12). All teachers should be trained to overcome their hidden biases. *Time.* https://time.com/3705454/teachers-biases-girls-education/

Chen, A. Y.-P. (2015, May). Educational inequality: An impediment to true democracy in the United States. *Sociology Study, 5*(5), 382–390.

Collier, V. P., & Thomas, W. P. (2004, Winter). The astounding effectiveness of dual language education for all. *NABE Journal of Research and Practice, 2*(1). www.berkeleyschools.net/wp-content/uploads/2011/10/TWIAstounding_Effectiveness_Dual_Language_Ed.pdf?864d7e

Cooperative Children's Book Center. (2023). *Books by and/or about Black, Indigenous and People of Color (all years).* https://ccbc.education.wisc.edu/literature-resources/ccbc-diversity-statistics/books-by-about-poc-fnn

Council on American-Islamic Relations. (2023). *2023 civil rights report: Progress in the shadow of prejudice.* Author. www.cair.com/wp-content/uploads/2023/04/progressintheshadowofprejudice-1.pdf

Cross, B. (2003). Learning or unlearning racism: Transferring teacher education curriculum to classroom practices. *Theory Into Practice, 42*(3), 203–209.

Cross, B. E. (2005). New racism, reformed teacher education, and the same ole' oppression. *Educational Studies: A Journal of the American Educational Studies Association, 38*(3), 263–274.

Dee, T., & Gershenson, S. (2017). *Unconscious bias in the classroom: Evidence and opportunities.* Stanford Center for Education Policy Analysis. http://hdl.handle.net/1961/auislandora:83263

Du Bois, W. E. B. (1903/1989). *The souls of Black folk.* Penguin.

Dulin-Keita, A., Hannon, L., Fernandez, J. R., & Cockerham, W. C. (2011, April). The defining moment: Children's conceptualization of race and experiences with racial discrimination. *Ethnic and Racial Studies, 34*(4), 662–682.

DuVernay, A. (Director). (2016). *13th* [Film]. Kandoo Films.

Elmasry, M. (2015, February 11). Chapel Hill shooting and western media bigotry. *Al Jazeera.* www.aljazeera.com/opinions/2015/2/11/chapel-hill-shooting-and-western-media-bigotry

Elsheikh, E., & Sisemore, B. (2021, September). *Islamophobia through the eyes of Muslims: Assessing perceptions, experiences, and impacts.* Othering & Belonging Institute. https://belonging.berkeley.edu/sites/default/files/2021-09/Islamophobia%20Through%20the%20Eyes%20of%20Muslims.pdf

Endres, D., & Gould, M. (2009). I am also in the position to use my whiteness to help them out: The communication of whiteness in service learning. *Western Journal of Communication, 73*(4), 418–436.

Essa, H. (n.d.). *Huda Essa: Ever American* (Curriculum materials). Teacher Created Materials.

Essa, H. (2016). *Teach us your name.* Author.

Essa, H. (2018). *Your name is the key!* TEDx Talk. www.ted.com/talks/huda_essa_your_name_is_the_key

Essa, H. (2019). *Common threads: Adam's day at the market.* Sleeping Bear Press.

Fairlie, R., Hoffmann, F., & Oreopoulos, P. (2014). A community college instructor like me: Race and ethnicity interactions in the classroom. *The American Economic Review, 104*(8), 2567–2591.

Fasching-Varner, K. (2012). *Working through whiteness: Examining white racial identity and profession with pre-service teachers.* Lexington Books.

Ferguson, R. F. (2003). Teachers' perceptions and expectations and the Black-White test score gap. *Urban Education, 38*(4), 460–507.

Flannery, M. E. (2015, September 9). When implicit bias shapes teacher expectations. *NEA Today.* www.nea.org/2015/09/09/when-implicit-bias-shapes-teacher-expectations

Gay, G. (2010). *Culturally responsive teaching: Theory, research, and practice.* Teachers College Press.

Geronimus, A. T., Hicken, M., Keene, D., & Bound, J. (2006, May). "Weathering" and age patterns of allostatic load scores among blacks and whites in the United States. *American Journal of Public Health, 96*(5), 826–833.

Gershenson, S., Holt, S. B., & Papageorge, N. W. (2016, June). Who believes in me? The effect of student–teacher demographic match on teacher expectations. *Economics of Education Review, 52,* 209–224.

Grissom, J. A., & Redding, C. (2016, January–March). Discretion and disproportionality: Explaining the underrepresentation of high-achieving students of color in gifted programs. *AERA Open, 2*(1).

Grissom, J. A., Rodriguez, L. A., & Kern, E. C. (2017). Teacher and principal diversity and the representation of students of color in gifted programs: Evidence from national data. *The Elementary School Journal, 117*(3), 396–422.

Gushue, G. V., & Constantine, M. G. (2007). Color-blind racial attitudes and white racial identity attitudes in psychology trainees. *Professional Psychology: Research and Practice, 38*(3), 321–328.

Hammond, Z. (2014). *Culturally responsive teaching and the brain: Promoting authentic engagement and rigor among culturally and linguistically diverse students.* Corwin.

Hancock, A. B., & Rubin, B. A. (2014). Influence of communication partner's gender on language. *Journal of Language and Social Psychology, 34*(1).

Harrington, T. (2018, April 6). Educator asks teachers to examine unconscious racial bias. *EdSource.* https://edsource.org/2018/closing-the-achievement-gap-requires-teachers-to-examine-their-unconscious-racial-bias-teacher-trainer-says/595408

Haviland, V. S. (2008). Things get glossed over: Rearticulating the silencing power of whiteness in education. *Journal of Teacher Education, 59*(1), 40–54.

Hirschfield, P. (2009). Another way out: The impact of juvenile arrests on high school dropout. *Sociology of Education, 82,* 368–393.

Hofstede, G., Hofstede, G. J., & Minkov, M. (2010). *Cultures and organizations: Software of the mind: Intercultural cooperation and its importance for survival* (2nd ed.). McGraw-Hill.

Hollie, S. (2017). *Culturally and linguistically responsive teaching and learning: Classroom practices for student success* (2nd ed.). Shell Educational Publishing.

Holt, S. B., & Gershenson, S. (2015, December). *The impact of teacher demographic representation on student attendance and suspensions* [Discussion paper no. 9554]. Institute for the Study of Labor. https://docs.iza.org/dp9554.pdf

Howard, T. C. (2010). *Why race and culture matter in schools: Closing the achievement gap in America's classrooms.* Teachers College Press.

Jackson, Y. (2011). *The pedagogy of confidence: Inspiring high intellectual performance in urban schools.* Teachers College Press.

Jhally, S., & Earp, J. (Directors). (2006). *Reel bad Arabs: How Hollywood vilifies a people* [Film]. Media Education Foundation.

Johnston, O., Wildy, H., & Shand, J. (2019). A decade of teacher expectations research 2008–2018: Historical foundations, new developments, and future pathways. *Australian Journal of Education, 63*(1), 44–73.

Jones, T. M., Fleming, C., Williford, A., & Research and Evaluation Team. (2020, December). Racial equity in academic success: The role of school climate and social emotional learning. *Children and Youth Services Review, 119.*

Kaur, H. (2023, May 1). Why some have mixed feelings about the terms Asian American and AAPI. *CNN.* www.cnn.com/2023/05/01/us/asian-american-aapi-terms-history-cec/index.html

Keengwe, J. (2010). Fostering cross cultural competence in preservice teachers through multicultural education experiences. *Early Childhood Education Journal, 38*(3), 197–204.

Khalifa, M. A., Gooden, M. A., & Davis, J. E. (2016). Culturally responsive school leadership: A synthesis of the literature. *Review of Educational Research, 86*(4), 1272–1311.

Kunstler, E., & Kunstler, S. (Directors). (2021). Who we are: A chronicle of racism in America [Film]. Sony Pictures Classics.

Ladson-Billings, G. (2009). *The dreamkeepers: Successful teachers of African American children* (2nd ed.). Jossey-Bass.

Lindsay, C. A., & Blom, E. (2017). *Diversifying the classroom: Examining the teacher pipeline.* Urban Institute. www.urban.org/features/diversifying-classroom-examining-teacher-pipeline

Lindsey, R. B., Nuri-Robins, K., & Terrell, R. D. (2003). *Cultural proficiency: A manual for school leaders* (2nd ed.). Corwin.

Martin, J. L. (2018). Factors contributing to microaggressions, racial battle fatigue, stereotype threat, and imposter phenomenon for nonhegemonic students: Implications for urban education. In G. C. Torino, D. P. Rivera, C. M. Capodilupo, K. L. Nadal, & D. W. Sue (Eds.), *Microaggression theory: Influence and implications* (pp. 102–120). Wiley.

Merriam-Webster. (n.d.). Privilege. In *Merriam-Webster.com dictionary.* Retrieved December 1, 2023, from https://www.merriam-webster.com/dictionary/privilege

MetLife. (2010, April). *The MetLife survey of the American teacher: Collaborating for student success.* https://files.eric.ed.gov/fulltext/ED509650.pdf

Mogahed, D., & Ikramullah, E. (2022, August). *American Muslim poll 2022: A politics and pandemic status report.* Institute for Social Policy and Understanding.

Moore, M. (Director). (2002). *Bowling for Columbine* [Film]. United Artists.

National Academies of Sciences, Engineering, and Medicine. (2018). *Sexual harassment of women: Climate, culture, and consequences in academic sciences, engineering, and medicine.* The National Academies Press.

National Center for Education Statistics (NCES). (2002). *Education longitudinal study of 2002* (ELS: 2002). U.S. Department of Education.

National Center for Education Statistics (NCES). (2021). *Digest of education statistics: Table 209.23: Number and percentage distribution of teachers in public elementary and secondary schools, by race/ethnicity and selected teacher and school characteristics: 2017–18*. U.S. Department of Education. https://nces.ed.gov/programs/digest/d21/tables/dt21_209.23.asp

National Center for Education Statistics (NCES). (2022). *Digest of education statistics: Table 315.20: Full-time faculty in degree-granting postsecondary institutions, by race/ethnicity, sex, and academic rank: Fall 2019, fall 2020, and fall 2021*. U.S. Department of Education. https://nces.ed.gov/programs/digest/d22/tables/dt22_315.20.asp

National Center for Education Statistics. (2023). Racial/ethnic enrollment in public schools. *Condition of education*. U.S. Department of Education, Institute of Education Sciences. https://nces.ed.gov/programs/coe/indicator/cge/racial-ethnic-enrollment

Ouazad, A. (2014, Summer). Assessed by a teacher like me: Race and teacher assessments. *Education Finance and Policy, 9*(3), 334–372.

Pager, D., Western, B., & Sugie, N. (2009, May). Sequencing disadvantage: Barriers to employment facing young black and white men with criminal records. *Annals of the American Academy of Political and Social Science, 623*(1), 195–213.

Pennington, J. L., Brock, C. H., & Ndura, E. (2012). Unraveling the threads of white teachers' conceptions of caring: Repositioning white privilege. *Urban Education, 47*(4), 743–775.

Perszyk, D. R., Lei, R. F., Bodenhausen, G. V., Richeson, J. A., & Waxman, S. R. (2019, May). Bias at the intersection of race and gender: Evidence from preschool-aged children. *Developmental Science, 22*(3). https://onlinelibrary.wiley.com/doi/epdf/10.1111/desc.12788

Peters, T., Margolin, M., Fragnoli, K., & Bloom, D. (2016, May). What's race got to do with it? Preservice teachers and white racial identity. *Current Issues in Education, 19*(1).

Phillips, S. F., & Pylkkänen, L. (2021, November 3). Composition within and between languages in the bilingual mind: MEG evidence from Korean/English bilinguals. *eNeuro, 8*(6).

Ruggles-Gere, A., Buehler, J., Dallavis, C., & Shaw-Haviland, V. (2009). A visibility project: Learning to see how preservice teachers take up culturally responsive pedagogy. *American Educational Research Journal, 46*(3), 816–852.

Samari, G. (2016, November). Islamophobia and public health in the United States. *American Journal of Public Health, 106*(11), 1920–1925. www.ncbi.nlm.nih.gov/pmc/articles/PMC5055770/

Saunders, S., & Kardia, D. (1997). *Creating inclusive college classrooms*. Center for Research on Learning and Teaching, University of Michigan. https://crlt.umich.edu/gsis/p3_1

Schlosser, E. (2017, December). *Race, socioeconomic status, and implicit bias: Implications for closing the achievement gap* [Dissertation]. The Graduate School, the College of Science and Technology, and the Center for Science and Mathematics Education, University of Southern Mississippi.

Sensoy, Ö., & DiAngelo, R. (2014). Respect differences? Challenging the common guidelines in social justice education. *Democracy and Education, 22*(2). https://democracyeducationjournal.org/cgi/viewcontent.cgi?article=1138&context=home

Shaheen, J. (2001). *Reel bad Arabs: How Hollywood vilifies a people.* Olive Branch Press.

Siebel Newsom, J. (Director). (2011). *Miss Representation* [Film]. Girls' Club Entertainment.

Staats, C., Capatosto, K., Wright, R. A., & Jackson, V. W. (2016). *State of the science: Implicit bias review: 2016 edition.* Kirwan Institute for the Study of Race and Ethnicity. https://culturalq.com/wp-content/uploads/2019/03/Kirwan-Institute-Implicit-Bias-2016-Report.pdf

Sue, D. W., Capodilupo, C. M., Torino, G. C., Bucceri, J. M., Holder, A. M. B., Nadal, K. L., & Esquilin, M. (2007). Racial microaggressions in everyday life: Implications for clinical practice. *American Psychologist, 62*(4), 271–286.

Tulshyan, R. (2022, March 8). We need to retire the term "microaggressions." *Harvard Business Review.* https://hbr.org/2022/03/we-need-to-retire-the-term-microaggressions

UNESCO. (2023). *The United Nations World Water Development Report 2023: Partnerships and cooperation for water.* Author. www.unesco.org/reports/wwdr/2023/en/download

U.S. Department of Education. (2015). *Talk, read and sing together every day! The benefits of being bilingual—A review for teachers and other early education program providers.* https://www2.ed.gov/documents/early-learning/talk-read-sing/bilingual-en.pdf

U.S. Department of Education Office for Civil Rights. (2014, March 21). *Civil rights data collection: Data snapshot (school discipline).* Author. https://ocrdata.ed.gov/assets/downloads/CRDC-School-Discipline-Snapshot.pdf

Van Den Bergh, L. (2010, June). The implicit prejudiced attitudes of teachers: Relations to teacher expectations and the ethnic achievement gap. *American Educational Research Journal, 47*(2), 497–527.

Vedantam, S. (Host). (2019, January 24). Creative differences [Audio podcast episode]. In *Hidden Brain.* Hidden Brain Productions. https://hiddenbrain.org/podcast/creative-differences

Walters, P. B. (2001). Educational access and the state: Historical continuities and discontinuities in racial inequality in American education. *Sociology of Education, 74,* 35–49.

Wright, A. C. (2015, November). *Teachers' perceptions of students' disruptive behavior: The effect of racial congruence and consequences for school suspension* [Unpublished manuscript]. University of California, Santa Barbara.

Zamudio, M. M. (2011). *Critical race theory matters.* Routledge.

Zelasko, N., & Antunez, B. (2000). *If your child learns in two languages: A parent's guide for improving educational opportunities for children acquiring English as a second language.* National Clearinghouse for Bilingual Education. https://files.eric.ed.gov/fulltext/ED447713.pdf

Index

The letter *f* following a page number denotes information contained in a figure.

About the Author

Huda Essa is the founder of Culture Links, LLC, a multiservice organization focused on providing a variety of high-quality, authentic cultural proficiency learning opportunities. She is a TEDx speaker and the author of the culturally authentic and responsive children's books *Teach Us Your Name* and *Common Threads: Adam's Day at the Market.*

Huda's thought-provoking learning opportunities and writing have positively influenced communities around the globe. She uses her extensive experience as a cultural proficiency consultant, former teacher, and multilingual education specialist to support organizations in successfully meeting their goals. Huda provides consulting, keynotes, and interactive learning opportunities for education professionals from preK–12 through higher education. Their collaborations help them develop practices that promote engagement, productivity, and overall achievement. Huda's award-winning work extends to supporting students directly as well as professionals in businesses, corporations, and nonprofit organizations. Her dedicated leadership is driven by the belief that cultural proficiency is a worthy, lifelong education benefiting people of all ages, social identities, and careers.

She can be reached via her website, www.culturelinksllc.com, and through her social media channels: on Facebook at www .facebook.com/culturelinksllc, LinkedIn at www.linkedin.com/in /huda-essa-27670932, and Instagram and X (formerly Twitter) at @culturelinksllc.

Related ASCD Resources

At the time of publication, the following resources were available (ASCD stock numbers appear in parentheses).

Aim High, Achieve More: How to Transform Urban Schools Through Fearless Leadership by Yvette Jackson and Veronica McDermott (#112015)

The Antiracist Roadmap to Educational Equity: A Systemwide Approach for All Stakeholders by Avis Williams and Brenda Elliott (#123023)

Cultivating Joyful Learning Spaces for Black Girls: Insights into Interrupting School Pushout by Monique W. Morris (Monique Couvson) (#121004)

Cultural Competence Now: 56 Exercises to Help Educators Understand and Challenge Bias, Racism, and Privilege by Vernita Mayfield (#118043)

Finding Your Leadership Soul: What Our Students Can Teach Us About Love, Care, and Vulnerability by Carlos R. Moreno (#123025)

Fix Injustice, Not Kids and Other Principles for Transformative Equity Leadership by Paul Gorski and Katy Swalwell (#120012)

The Innocent Classroom: Dismantling Racial Bias to Support Students of Color by Alexs Pate (#120025)

Keeping It Real and Relevant: Building Authentic Relationships in Your Diverse Classroom by Ignacio Lopez (#117049)

Leading Within Systems of Inequity in Education: A Liberation Guide for Leaders of Color by Mary Rice-Boothe (#123014)

Leading Your School Toward Equity: A Practical Framework for Walking the Talk by Dwayne Chism (#123003)

Literacy Is Liberation: Working Toward Justice Through Culturally Relevant Teaching by Kimberly N. Parker (#122024)

Restoring Students' Innate Power: Trauma-Responsive Strategies for Teaching Multilingual Newcomers by Louise El Yaafouri (#122004)

Stay and Prevail: Students of Color Don't Need to Leave Their Communities to Succeed by Nancy Gutiérrez and Roberto Padilla (#123006)

Support and Retain Educators of Color: 6 Principles for Culturally Affirming Leadership by Andrea Terrero Gabbadon (#123018)

Understanding Your Instructional Power: Curriculum and Language Decisions to Support Each Student by Tanji Reed Marshall (#122027)

For up-to-date information about ASCD resources, go to **www.ascd.org.** You can search the complete archives of *Educational Leadership* at **www.ascd.org/el.**

ASCD myTeachSource®

Download resources from a professional learning platform with hundreds of research-based best practices and tools for your classroom at http://myteach source.ascd.org/.

For more information, send an email to member@ascd.org; call 1-800-933-2723 or 703-578-9600; or write to Information Services, ASCD, 2800 Shirlington Road, Suite 1001, Arlington, VA 22206 USA.

ascd
whole child

The ASCD Whole Child approach is an effort to transition from a focus on narrowly defined academic achievement to one that promotes the long-term development and success of all children. Through this approach, ASCD supports educators, families, community members, and policymakers as they move from a vision about educating the whole child to sustainable, collaborative actions.

The Consciously Unbiased Educator relates to the **safe, engaged,** and **supported** tenets. *For more about the ASCD Whole Child approach, visit* ***www.ascd.org/wholechild.***

WHOLE CHILD
TENETS

1 HEALTHY
Each student enters school healthy and learns about and practices a healthy lifestyle.

2 SAFE
Each student learns in an environment that is physically and emotionally safe for students and adults.

3 ENGAGED
Each student is actively engaged in learning and is connected to the school and broader community.

4 SUPPORTED
Each student has access to personalized learning and is supported by qualified, caring adults.

5 CHALLENGED
Each student is challenged academically and prepared for success in college or further study and for employment and participation in a global environment.